you, me, and
- JESUS -

you, me, and -JESUS-

by

CLIFF RICHARD
with Bill Latham

HODDER AND STOUGHTON

LONDON SYDNEY AUCKLAND TORONTO

British Library Cataloguing in Publication Data

Richard, Cliff
   You, me and Jesus.
   1. Youth—Religious life.   2. Christian life
   I. Title
   248.8'3   BV4531.2
   ISBN 0-340-32902-5 (cased)
   ISBN 0-340-34628-0 (paperback)

First published in Great Britain 1983 (cased)
Second impression 1983.

First published in Great Britain 1983 (paperback)
Sixth impression 1984.

Published by Hodder and Stoughton Children's Books,
(a division of Hodder and Stoughton Ltd), Mill Road,
Dunton Green, Sevenoaks, Kent TN13 2YJ.

Printed in Great Britain by T. J. Press (Padstow) Ltd
Padstow, Cornwall.
Colour plates printed by Waterlows (Dunstable) Ltd

Designed by Graham Marks

Introduction

It wasn't intended to be like this — the book, I mean. The original idea was for a sort of *Cliff's Book of Favourite Bible Stories*. All very cosy bedtime reading. That was O.K. — but what was the point? There are a hundred and one different books of Bible stories already, and mine couldn't improve on those. And what about the Bible itself, come to that? The whole book is better than an anthology of bits and pieces.

No, if it was to be a Cliff collection, I wanted to explain why I'd chosen each section and what it meant to me. Just a sentence or two, I thought, on about fifteen really well-known parables or miracles of Jesus.

That's how it started. I ask you — how can you write only a couple of sentences, when even one Bible verse can be jammed full of contemporary meaning? And of course, when I started to make my selection, it wasn't the familiar diet of Sunday School stories that I picked on. It was the teaching and promises, the demands and implications, and all the other aspects of just being a Christian in the '80s. And as for fifteen... well, sorry, I overran a bit! But there's no way that even 100 extracts can cover the whole story, and I just hope I haven't presented too lop-sided a view of the gospel's essential ingredients.

I must make two things clear right at the beginning. Firstly, as far as I am concerned, the Bible is God's word to His creation, and for truth about Him — and about ourselves — it is one hundred per cent reliable. Its styles vary of course: some is history, some poetry, some parable, some narrative

— but all of it is inspired truth for our benefit. And that doesn't mean, by the way, that we have to part company with our intelligence as we read it. Nor must we blindly lift phrases and verses out of context to interpret as we please.

With my erratic schedule, it's difficult to set aside a regular time each day for Bible reading. Usually I try to do some study before going to bed, but sometimes I'm so clapped out that I manage no more than a verse or two and a sleepy prayer. All of us have to work out the best time and place for ourselves, and there are no rules. The important thing is to come to the Bible expecting to discover something relevant, vital and lasting. Paul explained it to Timothy like this: 'All Scripture is God-breathed and is useful for teaching, rebuking, correcting and training in righteousness, so that the man of God may be thoroughly equipped for every good work'.

That reminds me — the version of the Bible we've used is the New International Version. I'm using it increasingly at home and at church, and for me it successfully combines scholarship with a contemporary 'feel'. If you don't have a copy and want to refer to some of the passages I've chosen, it doesn't matter. It won't be all that different in your version.

The mention of scholarship brings me to the second thing you need to know. I'm no scholar and even less of a theologian. I'm a pop singer who became a Christian in the mid-sixties, and that's my only authority. What I've written is what I've learned and, I promise you, that's only a scratch on the surface. There's so much more, and what I'd love this book to be is a kind of appetite-whetter that will cause you to study the Bible for yourself and delve far deeper.

Maybe there'll be something here from the Bible, or possibly a comment I've written, that will cause you to think hard about your own situation or, more particularly, about your own relationship with God. That would be fantastic and I'd love to be of more help. Personally, of course, I just can't reply to your letters. I'm away a great deal and there aren't enough hours in the day. However, some Christian friends of mine, from a church in Guildford, Surrey, will help and, if you have a query or problem about the Bible or about the Christian faith, drop them a line. They don't guarantee to have all the answers, but they're willing to do their best. You can write c/o Philip Vogel, Sayers, Mount Pleasant, Guildford, Surrey, GU2 5HZ; but please remember to send a stamped addressed envelope for a reply.

Lastly, my thanks to Bill Latham, who put the book together while I was gallivanting around the world, and to Gill for the usual impeccable work on the steam typewriter. Thanks too for Yvonne's eagle-eye and for the encouragement given by my friends at Hodder and Stoughton to a very diffident author!
P.S. You should spot a few record titles of mine among the section headings. There should be 20 in all — but younger readers will need history books or a 'switched-on' grandma to find them!

CONTENTS

AND THEY CALLED HIM JESUS	15
ER, EXCUSE ME . . .	16
I'M NO HERO	18
IF ONLY THERE WERE PROOF	20
PROOF OF THE PUDDING	22
BLUE TURNS TO GREY	23
SOLID ROCK	24
A SONG AND DANCE	26
THROW DOWN A LINE	27
NO EASY OPTION	28
COME IN!	29
A HEART TRANSPLANT	30
SIN DOES MATTER	32
NOT SO CLEVER!	34
SENSE OF DIRECTION	35
POWER SUPPLY	36
IT'S WHO YOU KNOW THAT MATTERS	37
NO COMPARISON	38
A QUESTION OF PRIORITIES	39
AN OFFER YOU CAN REFUSE	40
I DO IT FOR JESUS	42
A ROCK AND A FORTRESS	44
LEARNING TO LEAN	45
NO DEBTS	46
START ALL OVER AGAIN	47
LIKE A LAMB TO THE SLAUGHTER	48
FRIEND IN HIGH PLACES	49
PLAIN MIND-BOGGLING	50
ALL MY LOVE	51
FIT TO BURST	52
WHEN JESUS DIED	54
CAN'T TAKE THE HURT ANY MORE	56
MOSES' POWERHOUSE	58
TAKING NO CHANCES!	60

YES, HE LIVES   61
GRUBBY HANDS   62
AN INCOME POLICY   64
MENTAL DIETS   66
MY KINDA LIFE   67
MUCH MORE VALUABLE   68
I'M THE LONELY ONE   70
LOOKING FORWARD TO TOMORROW   72
YOUR BIGGEST DECISION   73
IT'S ALL OVER   74
TEST YOUR TEMPERATURE   75
A REASON TO BELIEVE   76
NOT SO STUPID   78
FILTHY RAGS   79
WHAT MUST I DO?   80
BRAND NEW SONG   82
LOVE — THE REAL DEFINITION   84
WITH THE EYES OF A CHILD   86
WEIGHT-LIFTING   88
A HIGH COST   90
A LITTLE IN LOVE   91
LIVING IN HARMONY   92
ME AND MY SHADOW   94
PASS THE KIDNEYS!   96
EVERYTHING I NEED   98
WHO IS THIS MAN?   100
LIVING PROOF   102
RED HERRINGS!   104
SALT AND LIGHT   105
TWO KINDS OF FRUIT   106
CHRISTIAN IDENTIKIT   108
PRAYER CHANGES THINGS   109
NOT ME — JESUS!   110
YOU KNOW ME BETTER THAN I KNOW MYSELF   111

CAN'T ASK FOR ANYTHING MORE THAN YOU   112
DIFFERENT STANDARDS   114
ACTIONS SPEAK LOUDER . . .   116
WHAT'S IT WORTH?   117
WHAT WE WANT, OK?   118
ALL THAT GLITTERS . . .   119
POTTER'S CLAY   120
START AT HOME   121
A HARD LESSON   122
SORRY, I DON'T KNOW   123
YOU FEED THEM   124
POWER TO ALL OUR FRIENDS   126
EQUIPPED FOR BATTLE   127
AN INNER BATTLE   128
GROW UP!   130
THANK YOU VERY MUCH   131
NO MORE CRYING   132
AN ESCAPE ROUTE   133
CONFIDENT FAITH   134
WHO'S YOUR BOSS?   135
WHEN GOD DIDN'T LISTEN   136
A PERMANENT PARTNERSHIP   137
CONSTANTLY   138
MAKE YOUR MIND UP TIME   139
THE MAKER'S RULES   140
TIME IN BETWEEN   142
WEAK AND WOBBLY   144
CAN I BE SURE   146
A GRIM ALTERNATIVE   147
FAKES AND CHARLATANS   148
STRAIGHT FROM THE SHOULDER   149
A KEY QUESTION   150
SUBJECT INDEX   153
BIBLE INDEX   157

ILLUSTRATIONS

Frontis   (*Adrian Boot*)
1(a)   (*Dieter Zill*)
1(b)   (*Simon Fowler*)

1   A sweaty press conference in some overseas airport
    (*Helle Petersen*)

2   Heading for a fall . . .? (*Tom Gibson USA*)

3   We don't talk anymore (*Bill Latham*)

4   Masai warriors keep their spears sharp and lethal. I gave it
    back without arguing! (*Bill Latham*)

5   The Masai tribe's first (and possibly last) concert.
    (*Bill Latham*)

6   (*above*) Two great buddies of mine—Bill Latham and
    George Hoffman, Tear Fund's director (*Bill Latham*)
    (*below*) Some peace and quiet at my hideaway cottage in
    Wales is a rare treat (*Bill Latham*)

7   (*above & below*) It's amazing who you meet in the African
    bush! (*Bill Latham*)

8/9 Another of my unforgettable impromptu 'concerts'.
    (*Bill Latham*)

10 (*above & below*) What's this 'ere? (*Bill Latham*)

11 My gospel concert audiences paid for this high-powered
    machinery in an industrial training centre in Kenya.
    (*Bill Latham*)

12 The young ones—America and Africa. (*Cliff Richard/
    Bill Latham*)

13 Still in action after 25 years!

14 Which way to Sainsbury's? (*Bill Latham*)

15 There goes another 10p. (*Paul Cox—SLAG Photography*)

16 One of the 'governor' photographers as far as I'm concerned,
    'Bubi' Heilemann of BRAVO magazine in West Germany.

AND THEY CALLED HIM JESUS

But after he had considered this, an angel of the Lord appeared to him in a dream and said, 'Joseph son of David, do not be afraid to take Mary home as your wife, because what is conceived in her is from the Holy Spirit. She will give birth to a son, and you are to give him the name Jesus, because he will save his people from their sins.'

All this took place to fulfil what the Lord had said through the prophet: 'The virgin will be with child and will give birth to a son, and they will call him Immanuel' — which means, 'God with us'.

When Joseph woke up, he did what the angel of the Lord had commanded him and took Mary home as his wife. But he had no union with her until she gave birth to a son. And he gave him the name Jesus.

Matthew 1:20-25

I wonder whether the title of my book puts you off, or even makes you a bit wary? It's strange how people are prepared to talk endlessly about church and religion and even God, but mention Jesus and they clam up and get embarrassed. I guess it's because Jesus is so personal. You can waffle on about the latest religious theory without any risk of a practical challenge to your life or conscience, but focus on Jesus and it's well-nigh impossible to keep Him at arm's length. He confronts us with disturbing demands and decisions, and with a love that seems to lodge permanently in our subconscious. I suppose that can be uncomfortable.

But the name of Jesus mustn't be a deterrent to those who are open-minded, and if the book does nothing else, I'd love it to introduce Jesus to you as someone who, far from making life difficult or embarrassing or dreary, can cause it to be fantastically worthwhile and satisfying.

It's logical to begin with some verses about Jesus' birth, but it's His name that I want you to note especially. Matthew explains that it means 'Saviour', just like the Old Testament name of Joshua. Add to that His title 'Immanuel' — 'God with us' — and you have enough food for thought to digest for a week.

There was a time when Thomas recognised the truth about Jesus, and fell at His feet and called Him, 'My Lord and my God'. Maybe you haven't reached that point yet and Jesus remains an enigma — obviously crucial in the lives of Christians, but irrelevant and unreal to you. Where is the line between truth and make-believe? Could a little baby really be the same God who created the universe? And who did He come to save and from what? Of course there are questions, but I know there are answers — good, positive ones at that. So how about us getting together over the next few pages — you and me and Jesus?

'ER, EXCUSE ME ...'

'So now, go. I am sending you to Pharaoh to bring my people the Israelites out of Egypt.'

But Moses said to God, 'Who am I, that I should go to Pharaoh and bring the Israelites out of Egypt?'

And God said, 'I will be with you. And this will be the sign to you that it is I who have sent you: When you have brought the people out of Egypt, you will worship God on this mountain.'

Moses said to God, 'Suppose I go to the Israelites and say to them, "The God of your fathers has sent me to you," and they ask me, "What is his name?" Then what shall I tell them?'

God said to Moses, 'I am who I am. This is what you are to say to the Israelites: "I AM has sent me to you."'

Moses answered, 'What if they do not believe me or listen to me and say, "The LORD did not appear to you"?'

Then the LORD said to him, 'What is that in your hand?'

'A staff,' he replied.

I used to think that the Bible was **made** up entirely of Superman characters — not a bit like me and a trifle too good to be true. Some of them seemed so remote that they might well have been some green ET monsters with furry feet!

Yet, when I actually started to read the Bible for myself, I had a shock. Even some of those heavyweight Old Testament guys began to emerge as regular down-to-earth people who reacted and behaved in very human and fallible ways.

Take Moses, for instance. Fantastic leader though he was, I reckon he'd get an A-level in Excuses. The fact is that he didn't want to do what he knew he should. He believed in God all right — that was no problem. The crunch came in doing what God wanted and going where God was leading. After all, he just wasn't good enough; he didn't have it in him.

Read through Moses' excuses again and I bet they'll ring bells. 'Who am I, Lord?' 'I'm not the religious sort.' 'Suppose they think I'm crazy.' 'I've got this

The LORD said, 'Throw it on the ground.'

Mose threw it on the ground and it became a snake, and he ran from it.

Moses said to the LORD, 'O Lord, I have never been eloquent, neither in the past nor since you have spoken to your servant. I am slow of speech and tongue.'

The LORD said to him, 'Who gave man his mouth? Who makes him deaf or dumb? Who gives him sight or makes him blind? Is it not I, the LORD? Now go; I will help you speak and will teach you what to say.'

But Moses said, 'O Lord, please send someone else to do it.'

Exodus 3:10-14; 4:1-3, 10-13

problem.' 'Please, Lord, choose **someone** else.' I admit it, I can identify with Moses all too easily. And some of those objections still cross my mind, particularly when I have to leave home on a wet Saturday maybe to slog up the motorway for a church meeting 200 miles away. 'Why me? Aren't I busy enough without having to give up a free day?'

But notice that each time Moses threw up an obstacle God dealt with it until eventually he learned that, if God called him to do something, He'd give him the strength and the ability to do it. In other words, He never expects or demands the impossible and, when we try to excuse ourselves from facing up to God's will, it isn't ourselves we underrate, but God's ability to work in us. When Paul wrote 'I can do all things through Christ who strengthens me', it wasn't some optimistic theory he was spouting, but a truth which he had discovered actually worked in practice.

I'M NO HERO

*I do not understand what I do. For
what I want to do I do not do, but
what I hate I do. And if I do what I do
not want to do, I agree that the law is
good. As it is, it is no longer I myself
who do it, but it is sin living in me. I
know that nothing good lives in me,
that is, in my sinful nature. For I have
the desire to do what is good, but I
cannot carry it out. For what I do is
not the good I want to do; no, the evil I
do not want to do — this I keep on
doing. Now if I do what I do not want
to do, it is no longer I who do it, but it
is sin living in me that does it.*

Romans 7:15-20

Let's scotch the idea once and for all that Christianity is reserved for a bunch of
goody-goodies. When a person becomes a Christian, he doesn't get
dehumanised. Nor is he transformed into some pious robot immune from the
temptations and pitfalls which beset others. It annoys me no end when a
newspaper makes headlines from a story about a Christian who slips up and
does something wrong. The 'angle' isn't the crime; it's the fact that a Christian
has committed it! Of course a Christian shouldn't do wrong, of course his aim
should be to reflect Jesus and to be His ambassador, but he doesn't have a built-
in sin exterminator, and sometimes he falls flat on his face. 'Tut tut — and he
calls himself a Christian,' gloats the world. 'So much for Christianity.' As
though we can judge the Christian faith by any one of its followers! That would
be far too easy, as well as being disastrous. It was Gandhi, the great Indian
leader, who is reported to have said that the worst thing about Christianity is
Christians.

It troubles me to think that, if I were to ever get into some scrape, the press
would have a field day. If I even got a speeding fine, I reckon it would be on the
placards. Not because it's Cliff Richard, but because it's Cliff Richard, the
Christian. If I'm discredited then, in the eyes of many, so is all that I stand for.

While the last thing in the world I want is to let Jesus down, let me say here and now that Christianity doesn't stand or fall by me or any other Christian. It's Jesus that it depends upon. Pick holes in Jesus and you undermine Christianity. Pick holes in Cliff Richard and all you do is underline my humanity.

Understand that I'm not excusing failure. The Christian's role is to be on the winning side, on the side of right, and to be like Christ. In this life, however, he's far from perfect. Paul must be one of the most outstanding of all Christians, yet his experience was of constant tussle. Things he didn't want to do he found himself doing, and the things he knew he should have done he left undone. Personally, I find that a massive encouragement. I couldn't live under the pressure of having to achieve one hundred per cent perfection. In fact, if that's what Christianity demanded, I'd pack it in now as a bad job.

The difference between the Christian and the non-Christian is that, when the non-Christian fails, he has nowhere to go for peace of mind. When the Christian fails, and regrets it, he can hold his head up again, assured that God will already have forgiven and forgotten. Society will mark the slate; God will wipe it clean.

IF ONLY THERE WERE PROOF

*Now Thomas (called Didymus),
one of the Twelve, was not with the
disciples when Jesus came. When the
other disciples told him that they had
seen the Lord, he declared, 'Unless I
see the nail marks in his hands and put
my finger where the nails were, and
put my hand into his side, I will not
believe it.'*

*A week later his disciples were in
the house again, and Thomas was
with them. Though the doors were
locked, Jesus came and stood among
them, and said, 'Peace be with you!'
Then he said to Thomas, 'Put your
finger here; see my hands. Reach out
your hand and put it into my side.
Stop doubting and believe.'*

*Thomas answered, 'My Lord and
my God!'*

*Then Jesus told him, 'Because you
have seen me, you have believed;
blessed are those who have not seen
and yet have believed.'*

John 20:24-29

Everyone can relate to Thomas. Doubting Thomas, he's been labelled, as
though it was some slur on his character. But how would you have reacted?
Would you have believed the other disciples? Would you have accepted that
they had seen Jesus alive, just a few days after He had been executed and
buried? It was a tall story, all right. In his heart, I reckon Thomas would have
loved to believe it. If only it were true that Jesus was alive and that there was a
future with Him. But how could He be? All Thomas's logic and common-sense
told him that death was the end. And he'd need some hefty proof to convince
him otherwise.

Of course we relate to Thomas. It was a natural response and there must be millions like him who think 'if only' . . . If only I could be sure there was a God who loved me . . . If only I could be certain it isn't one huge hoax . . . If only there were proof.

I'm often asked about doubts and I know it's easy to give the impression that everything is neatly buttoned up. Personally I have few doubts about the reality of God and the truth of Christianity. What I do have are scores of 'don't knows', areas that I don't begin to understand. Pain and suffering, for instance, raise all sorts of question-marks. I don't know why God permits certain events, calamities and disasters, which destroy and injure and maim. I don't understand, but I still believe.

Thomas was privileged. He was given the proof he needed to recognise Jesus as his Lord and his God. It was proof reserved for him. No-one else had the opportunity to actually feel the marks of the nails in Jesus' body. It was a personal encounter which Thomas would have carried with him for the rest of his life. Very few since Thomas have been given any tangible proof — although down the centuries and still today there are those privileged to witness dramatic miracles of healing, which have to be physical evidence of God's activity.

For most of us, I guess, there is no tangible proof. 'Blessed are those who have not seen but have believed', said Jesus. Thomas could always look back to an actual physical encounter. Personally, I can't recall a meeting like that, but there was a time when by faith I reached out my hand to Jesus, and near y twenty years of subsequent Christian experience have given me all the assurance I need. Its validity of course is for me and for me alone. There's nothing I can prove to you and my experience will convince you of nothing. You have to stretch out your own hand.

PROOF OF THE PUDDING

I waited patiently for the LORD;
he turned to me and heard my
cry.
He lifted me out of the slimy pit,
out of the mud and mire;
he set my feet on a rock
and gave me a firm place to
stand.
He put a new song in my mouth,
a hymn of praise to our God.
Many will see and fear and put
their trust in the LORD.

Blessed is the man who makes the
LORD his trust,
who does not look to the proud,
to those who turn aside to false
gods.
Many, O LORD my God, are the
wonders you have done.
The things you planned for us no-
one can recount to you:
were I to speak and tell of them,
they would be too many to
declare.

Psalm 40:1-5

It probably sounds a bit quaint, all this about slimy pits and mud and mire. In fact it's David's poetic way of telling us how radically God had changed and restored his life. Nothing unique, but little short of a miracle for the person concerned.

At one stage David's life was a mess. Nothing seemed secure or reliable. No-one had given him real peace or stability. Days were lonely and empty.

And then came the change. God took priority in David's life. Instead of slippery mud underfoot, there was firm rock. Instead of feeling trapped and claustrophobic, there was freedom and fresh air.

It's difficult to explain to those who are cynical, but then we're not always bound to explain. For David it was sufficient to say, 'This is what God has done.' A bit like the blind man who was cured by Jesus: 'All I know,' he said, 'is that once I was blind, but now I can see.'

Some of you may have that 'eye-opener' to come. When it does, you'll understand about 'the new song' God puts in your mouth. Some years ago, a friend wrote a book about me and called it *New Singer, New Song*. That was a great title because becoming a Christian not only changed me, it changed what I had to say. What about the song? You'll have to come to one of my gospel concerts and judge for yourself!

BLUE TURNS TO GREY

And we know that in all things God works for the good of those who love him, who have been called according to his purpose. For those God foreknew he also predestined to be conformed to the likeness of his Son, that he might be the firstborn among many brothers. And those he predestined, he also called; those he called, he also justified; those he justified, he also glorified.

Romans 8:28-30

One of the hardest promises for me to accept, let alone understand, is this one about 'all things working together for good to those who love God'. There seems to be a naive belief that celebrities — particularly showbiz stars — live in a permanent glamour world, where the skies are always blue and the days are full of fun and parties. Of course that's nonsense (apart from a few who believe their own press hand-outs and they're in big trouble!). I can assure you that my days are much the same as yours, and every now and again circumstances crop up that are difficult or painful. It's then that I find myself asking how on earth this fantastic promise can actually be true. How can any good possibly result from a mess like this?

I can only tell you what I tell myself, and that is that God doesn't lie. His Word is more reliable than my feelings. So I accept it and believe it by faith — not blind thoughtless faith, but a logical conclusion based on the fundamental premise that God really is King of Kings and Lord of Lords and, as the Psalmist says, 'holds all things in the palm of His hand'.

What's more, my experience backs up that faith. With hindsight, I can vouch for the fact that good has somehow squeezed itself from circumstances that were grim at the time. Disappointments, relationship break-ups, even illnesses which were painful to endure and difficult to interpret as anything but bad, have turned out to be invaluable in terms of equipping me to cope with the present and enabling me to identify more easily with the permanently sick and disabled.

It's easy to say, I know, but if you're a Christian going through some really tough experience right now, remember this principle. It's not all bad. From somewhere, for someone, there will be benefit and good, not despite your circumstances, but because of them.

SOLID ROCK

'Therefore everyone who hears these words of mine and puts them into practice is like a wise man who built his house on the rock. The rain came down, the streams rose, and the winds blew and beat against that house; yet it did not fall, because it had its foundation on the rock. But everyone who hears these words of mine and does not put them into practice is like a foolish man who built his house on sand. The rain came down, the streams rose, and the winds blew and beat against that house, and it fell with a great crash.'

When Jesus had finished saying these things, the crowds were amazed at his teaching, because he taught as one who had authority, and not as their teachers of the law.

Matthew 7:24-29

A friend of mine 'phoned me recently and told me very calmly that he and his family were having to move out of their house for six months, because it was collapsing. A huge crack had suddenly appeared across the bathroom wall and the builders had diagnosed dodgy foundations. Unless urgent work was done, the whole place was in danger of total collapse. Now, if it had occurred in some earthquake-prone zone, I could understand it, but this was Bournemouth of all places and, as I write, my friends are stripping their home of literally everything — furniture, carpets, the lot — and moving into a rented apartment. A domestic disaster, and all because of a bad foundation.

Jesus' story makes such good sense that I can't imagine anyone disputing it. Foundations are critical and, whether we consciously think about it or not, all of us build our lives on some kind of base — parental influence, friends, education, environment and so on. Obviously the more stable the influences the better, but the fact is that there isn't much we can do about them if they're not. That's our bad fortune.

There is a foundation, however, that we can determine ourselves, and a more reliable and permanent one for our lives I can't imagine. That's Jesus, and I know from my own experience that, when stormy times have come — and Christians aren't immune to them — and I've been battered around by this and that, Jesus has been a really stabilising factor.

To be quite honest, if it weren't for Him, I suspect my life would have been on the way to being a bit of a heap by now. There would certainly have been an ominous crack or two!

A SONG AND DANCE

'Come, let us sing for joy to the
LORD;
let us shout aloud to the Rock of
our salvation.
Let us come before him with
thanksgiving and extol him with
music and song.
For the LORD is the great God, the
great King above all gods.

In his hand are the depths of the
earth,
and the mountain peaks belong to
him.
The sea is his, for he made it, and his
hands formed the dry land.
Come, let us bow down in
worship,
let us kneel before the LORD
our Maker;
for he is our God
and we are the people of his
pasture,
the flock under his care.

Psalm 95:1-7

Do you have those times when you get so excited about something you reckon you'll burst? I get the feeling that David wasn't too far off explosion point when he wrote this. God was so real to him, so great, so fantastic, that he wanted to shout it from the rooftops.

Sometimes it's right to come to God very quietly and humbly, but not always. And today many Christians are finding a whole new freedom and joy in worshipping their Lord. And, when you think about it, if we can't get worked up about God, who created us and the universe, who is Lord of Lords and King of Kings, and yet who knows us and loves us, then surely we'll never enthuse about anything.

Do you see the point? On the one hand, God is so vast and majestic that my puny little mind can't begin to understand Him. But, if that was all, what a remote, distant, irrelevant God He would be. The wonder is that He's no way distant because, through Jesus, we can actually know Him and relate to Him like a child to a father. Even David, who knew nothing about Jesus, wasn't frightened by God's greatness. He was all for singing and shouting about it from sheer gratitude. Come to think of it, he might just have had a ball at one of my gospel concerts! As a backing vocalist, of course!

THROW DOWN A LINE

Here is a trustworthy saying that deserves full acceptance: Christ Jesus came into the world to save sinners — of whom I am the worst. But for that very reason I was shown mercy so that in me, the worst of sinners, Christ Jesus might display his unlimited patience as an example for those who would believe on him and receive eternal life. Now to the King eternal, immortal, invisible, the only God, be honour and glory for ever and ever. Amen.

1 Timothy 1:15-17

There are certain words that, although perfectly good in themselves, get abused and misused by society until they communicate something quite different from the original meaning. That sounds a bit pompous, I know, but take the two words in this section, 'save sinners', for instance. The sentence has a fantastic meaning, yet I know the phrase could well conjure up a caricature of some religious crank with a glint in his eye, waving a Bible under someone's nose and demanding, 'Are you saved?'

Let's forget the caricature. It gets in the way of our understanding and it's unfair anyway, because I don't think many balanced Christians would act so daft. I tell you, if I approached my band like that, they'd run a mile! When we use the word 'saved', we either mean saved from something or saved to or for something, and both ideas are there in the Bible. Jesus' death on the cross saves us *from* the consequences of our sin. According to the Bible, sin is desperately serious. It spoils our lives and separates us from God.

'The wages (or the results) of sin are death,' writes Paul. If we trust Jesus and accept His offer of new life, however, that sin and its results are wiped out. Totally and permanently erased, and we're saved from all prospect of an eternity away from God.

But there's the opposite side, too. We're saved *to* enjoy a whole new lifestyle, which is full and fruitful. We're saved *to* be salt and light in God's world — I've mentioned that elsewhere — and we're saved *to* be God's children, to live with Him for always for His pleasure.

It's a pity that we've poked fun at the idea of being saved, because it's what Jesus came to make possible. And there shouldn't be anything cranky or embarrassing about it. It boils down to whether we recognise our need for a Saviour, and accept Him, or prefer to go it alone.

NO EASY OPTION

Then Jesus said to his disciples, 'If anyone would come after me, he must deny himself and take up his cross and follow me. For whoever wants to save his life will lose it, but whoever loses his life for me will find it. What good will it be for a man if he gains the whole world, yet forfeits his soul? Or what can a man give in exchange for his soul? For the Son of Man is going to come in his Father's glory with his angels, and then he will reward each person according to what he has done.'

Matthew 16:24-27

You'll have found out, like me, that people have all sorts of weird and wonderful notions about what being a Christian really is. Some reckon it's a cosy escape route from the real world; others that it's a kind of convenient insurance policy against what might be in store after we die. But the one that really gets up my nose is that Christianity is for the weak and the spineless — for the chinless wonders of this world. It only goes to show of course how badly informed the critics are, for, as Christians know all too well, the actual living out of the Christian life is anything but a soft option. In this section from Matthew's Gospel, Jesus warns that it would be quite the reverse — demanding, sometimes to the point of ultimate self-sacrifice, as it was of course for many of those early followers who went to their execution rather than deny Jesus.

For boys and girls, it's particularly tough to cope with the classroom know-alls, who foolishly put down the Christian faith as something weak and soppy. If only they could meet some of those incredibly dedicated and committed Christian people that I've encountered in Africa and Asia, who have been working in ghastly circumstances of disease and poverty, not because they enjoy it but because they're being obedient.

Firstly, then, don't be put off by the mockers. I guess one of my Christian nurse friends, doing a four-year stint in Bangladesh or Somalia, demonstrates enough guts to knock the 'sissy' argument on the head once and for all. But secondly, and more important, if you're thinking about making a Christian commitment, don't bank on some magic wand that makes problems and hardships vanish. They won't, and there's certainly no magic wand or formula. God doesn't operate like that, and He never promises to get His people round the problems. What He does promise is to get us through them!

COME IN!

Here I am! I stand at the door and knock. If anyone hears my voice and opens the door, I will go in and eat with him, and he with me.

To him who overcomes, I will give the right to sit with me on my throne, just as I overcame and sat down with my Father on his throne. He who has an ear, let him hear what the Spirit says to the churches.

Revelation 3:20-22

This is probably a passage that has more nostalgic significance for me than any other — and I suspect there are quite a few like me. It was this picture of Jesus standing at the door of my life and knocking to come in that brought about my commitment to Christianity back in the mid-sixties. For two years or more, I had been arguing, discussing and sometimes just chatting about Christianity with all sorts of people. Sometimes the answers and the people irritated me, but the whole question of God and Jesus bugged me and I needed to know what, if anything, was true. Besides that, my life wasn't what it should have been. In one sense I had everything — money, fame, success, the lot. What I didn't get was peace of mind and, I promise you, that counts for more than anything.

So it wasn't as though I'd read this passage from the last book of the Bible for the first time, but somehow, as I was lying on a bed in North London, the situation became all very personal. Someone had asked me a question that really got under my skin. 'O.K.', they said, 'You think you know it all. How do you know you're a Christian?' And, to be honest, I hadn't a clue. It was true I'd read a lot, got all manner of information in my head about the Bible, but I didn't *know* I was a Christian. Because, as I realised in my friend's house, I wasn't one. I knew *about* Jesus but the was no personal encounter, no one-to-one relationship. There was a lot in my head but no-one in my life.

And then I read Revelation 3:20 and saw that Jesus wanted me, if I wanted Him.

I've said it often, but there were no voices in my ear or flashing lights, nothing remotely supernatural or dramatic. Quite simply I prayed that Jesus would come into my life, be my Lord and my Saviour, and make me new. The next morning I woke, not feeling particularly different, except for one critical detail. Now I could answer the question: I knew I was a Christian, because I had responded to Christ's knocking, and He wouldn't lie. Jesus was in my life.

A HEART TRANSPLANT

Meanwhile, Saul was still breathing out murderous threats against the LORD'S disciples. He went to the high priest and asked him for letters to the synagogues in Damascus, so that if he found any there who belonged to the Way, whether men or women, he might take them as prisoners to Jerusalem. As he neared Damascus on his journey, suddenly a light from heaven flashed around him. He fell to the ground and heard a voice say to him, 'Saul, Saul, why do you persecute me?'

'Who are you, LORD?' Saul asked.

'I am Jesus, whom you are persecuting,' he replied. 'Now get up and go into the city, and you will be told what you must do.'

Acts 9:1-6

Conversions to Christianity which result in drastically changed lives must be really hard to explain away. Paul's change of heart on the Damascus road was a classic turn-about, although not unique. Admittedly it was sudden, dramatic and radical in its physical after-effects but, throughout the centuries, there have been similar accounts of people meeting Jesus 'out of the blue', as it were, and finding their lives completely changed as a result. God deals with different people in different ways, and whereas my own conversion was a relatively quiet unsensational business — I've described it in another section — Paul must have needed quite a hefty jolt to make him change course. Saul, as he was known before his conversion, was a proud and staunch Jew and was determined to wipe out every trace of this new Christian message that was spreading like wildfire. It was like a personal crusade. At all costs Christianity had to be stopped, even if it meant death to those who proclaimed it. Time, inconvenience and even danger didn't matter to Saul two hoots. He was set on his course, incensed with anger, and genuine and sincere about the rightness of his cause. From our perspective we can see how easy it was to be sincerely wrong.

Not once had Saul considered Jesus with an open mind. His background, culture and beliefs all combined to create one colossal prejudice. Jesus was a charlatan and His followers were dangerous fools.

And all the while God had plans for Saul to become Christianity's greatest missionary and teacher. Can you imagine his reaction if someone had told him? He'd have blown his top!

There is no scientific explanation for what happened on Saul's Damascus journey. Obviously it was God who intervened. Clearly it was an experience that shattered Saul's pride and arrogance. For three years afterwards he was led and cared for by other Christians and, during that time, I imagine he was preparing himself for his extraordinary new role and getting to know Jesus as his Lord and Saviour, instead of as a hated and feared enemy.

The readjustment and re-orientation must have been enormous but, at the end of it, Paul emerged a new person. Can you imagine how the jaws of his old friends, and of the Christians too, must have gaped? How could a person change character so much? Sure, there was still the steely determination in the eye, but now it was all for Jesus and it seemed to be tempered with a compassion and a love that were never there before. It was as though there had been a complete change of heart.

Paul's old colleagues must have talked together and wondered, particularly if they read their Old Testament. 'I will give you a new heart and put a new spirit in you,' says God in Ezekiel. 'I will remove from you your heart of stone and give you a heart of flesh.' They may have said nothing but secretly they must have been impressed. As I said, you can disagree with a theory but how do you explain a new heart?

It makes you think twice about heart transplants. It seems they've been happening for some time!

SIN *DOES* MATTER

Achan replied, 'It is true! I have sinned against the Lord, the God of Israel. This is what I have done: When I saw in the plunder a beautiful robe from Babylonia, two hundred shekels of silver and a wedge of gold weighing fifty shekels, I coveted them and took them. They are hidden in the ground inside my tent, with the silver underneath.'

So Joshua sent messengers, and they ran to the tent, and there it was, hidden in his tent, with the silver underneath. They took the things from the tent, brought them to Joshua and all the Israelites and spread them out before the Lord.

Then Joshua, together with all Israel, took Achan son of Zerah, the silver, the robe, the gold wedge, his sons and daughters, his cattle, donkeys and sheep, his tent and all that he had, to the Valley of Achor. Joshua said, 'Why have you brought this disaster on us? The Lord will bring disaster on you today.'

Then all Israel stoned him, and after they had stoned the rest, they burned them.

Joshua 7:20-25

Not all of the Bible is comfortable reading. Far from it. Old Testament justice was often brutal and harsh and I admit I don't always find it easy to understand. But we can't 'skip' parts of the Bible because they're difficult or unpalatable. All of it is there for a purpose and contributes to the over-all picture. The lesson of Achan is like one small piece of the Bible jigsaw and is there to balance and complement the rest.

So what is the lesson? On the surface, it seems that the punishment outweighed the crime. After all, it was only a minor piece of dishonesty. No-one was hurt and no-one would miss a little silver and gold!

Let me tell you what I learn. Firstly, you can hide nothing from God. Achan naively thought that nobody knew. The loot was concealed under his tent and it might have been the perfect crime, but he didn't bargain for what effect it would have on the people. Suddenly things began to go wrong. Battles were lost and morale fell apart. Something was spoiling that special relationship that the Israelites had with God, and it was Joshua, the people's leader, who discerned the fault. Someone had disobeyed. That unique covenant that the Jews had made with the Lord had been broken, because somewhere in the camp there was sin. And where there was sin, God couldn't bless. That's lesson number two: sin and God's blessing don't go together — it's true in a person's life and, more mysteriously, it's often true in a group or church. Sin hinders God from working.

So Joshua, with insight from God and some detective's intuition, rooted out Achan and his theft was uncovered. And what followed was a total wiping out of everyone and everything associated with him. If it seems unfair, understand this — that sin is serious. The theft was not massive, but it mattered, and God couldn't condone it.

There's a tendency today to be light on sin, to make excuses for it, and even sometimes to justify it. The story of Achan gives me God's perspective and, uncomfortable though it is, I find that disobedience and sin — mine included — is unacceptable to Him. Like a cancer which will destroy the whole body, it has to be located and removed.

NOT SO CLEVER!

While Jesus was having dinner at Matthew's house, many tax collectors and 'sinners' came and ate with him and his disciples. When the Pharisees saw this, they asked his disciples, 'Why does your teacher eat with tax collectors and "sinners"?'

On hearing this, Jesus said, 'It is not the healthy who need a doctor, but the sick. But go and learn what this means: "I desire mercy, not sacrifice." For I have not come to call the righteous, but sinners.'

Matthew 9:10-13

It's never worried me when cynics say that Christianity is a crutch or prop for those who need one. They're right — it is a prop and I do need one. I'm the first to admit it. Christianity has little to offer, in this life at least, to the self-sufficient and to those totally convinced and confident of their own abilities to see them through.

Personally, I don't regard myself as that competent and to tap spiritual resources for support is no admission of weakness. Jesus said it so simply — He didn't come for those who think they can cope. His love and salvation are for those who know they can't. If someone has no sense of need, why turn to Jesus? Admittedly, I've known some who've become Christians because of intellectual conviction, some through the impact of a dramatic sunset or natural beauty, but for the majority, I'm sure, Jesus becomes relevant when we admit that we're not 'righteous', that we're not that brilliant and that we're not in fact the totally 'together' person we like to project.

One thing's for sure. Our public image is invariably streets ahead of that private character we keep under wraps. Don't let it bug you that Jesus might be a prop. The fact is that society desperately needs one. What are cigarettes, alcohol, drugs, and umpteen other addictions, if they're not to make life more tolerable? Society's props tend to be fallible, deceptive and temporary, and cost much in terms of money and health. Life investment in Jesus is also costly but the return is fantastic, and your support is guaranteed, totally dependable and for ever. There's a verse tucked away in the book of Deuteronomy that says, 'The eternal God is your refuge, and underneath are the everlasting arms.'

Personally, I choose His support every time.

SENSE OF DIRECTION

But you, man of God, flee from all this, and pursue righteousness, godliness, faith, love, endurance and gentleness. Fight the good fight of the faith. Take hold of the eternal life to which you were called when you made your good confession in the presence of many witnesses. In the sight of God, who gives life to everything, and of Christ Jesus, who while testifying before Pontius Pilate made the good confession, I charge you to keep this commandment without spot or blame until the appearing of our Lord Jesus Christ.

1 Timothy 6:11-14

Here it is again — in case you're in any doubt — the Christian life is tough and demanding. Look at some of these directions that Paul gives to young Timothy. He's to flee or turn his back on things that are evil. He's to pursue righteousness and godliness and so on. He's to fight for his faith, and must take hold of and start using the new life God has given him.

It's all far removed from just a weekly jaunt to church, and I reckon I'd be tempted to pack it all in as a pretty hopeless, one-sided affair if it weren't for the fact that this huge God, the King of Kings and Lord of Lords, knows how inept I am when it comes to good resolutions, and actually weighs in alongside me. That stacks the odds very differently, because while on my own I'd make a hash of fleeing and fighting and pursuing, God and me together — well, that's another story! My role as His partner is to get in there and be sure of whose side I'm on, and equally sure of which direction I'm going.

Hundreds of careers in show-business sink midstream because artists don't know which direction they're heading. They flounder around, trying their hand at this and that, and never become expert at anything. Christians must know what they're chasing, what track they're on. If we're not sure what we're pursuing, it's a certainty that we'll never catch it!

POWER SUPPLY

If you love me, you will obey what I command. And I will ask the Father, and he will give you another Counsellor to be with you for ever — the Spirit of truth. The world cannot accept him, because it neither sees him nor knows him. But you know him, for he lives with you and will be in you. I will not leave you as orphans; I will come to you. Before long, the world will not see me any more, but you will see me. Because I live, you also will live.

John 14:15-19

Imagine the disciples — geared up to take on the world, but depending totally on Jesus to show them how. Without Him they had nothing — no weapons, no skills, no strategy, not even much intelligence. But *with* Jesus they knew anything was possible. Certainly there was the most fantastic new future ahead. Their role was to stick close to His heels, to follow where He led, and to do as He directed.

And now their minds were trying to grasp a whole new concept and it was hard. Jesus was going to leave them! It didn't matter how or why at that moment. The point was that, despite His going away, the disciples weren't being abandoned. They weren't expected to go it alone under their own feeble steam, because God would come to them in a new way, and actually live in their lives to make them new people with new power and new resources. We know from the story that at first the disciples understood very little of all that. It must have sounded very weird and improbable and, as far as we know, provided little by way of encouragement or comfort. That is, until the day of Pentecost some weeks later, when God burst into the disciples' lives in an extraordinary way, to change them from timid, disillusioned failures into men whose courage and testimony changed the course of history.

I don't understand how God, the Holy Spirit, works in a person's life today. All I can say from my own experience is that, when I became a Christian, God didn't leave me to go it alone. Cliff Richard, left to his own resources, couldn't begin to live the Christian life. It would be a sick joke. So when I made my commitment to God, He made a commitment to me and, by a miracle, — for that's what it has to be — sent the Holy Spirit to be part of my life and to work in me gently and gradually as I allow Him over the years.

As I say, I can't analyse the Holy Spirit. I can't touch Him and I can't see Him, but I know He's active. I see Him at work, not only in my life but, more obviously, in the lives of many of my friends. There's just no other way I can account for changes in personalities and characters. Sometimes the Holy Spirit works dramatically and brings special gifts of healing and speaking in strange tongues. Sometimes He works quietly but equally profoundly, enabling God's children to mature and to grow into useful servants.

If you're a Christian, don't be anxious. God's given you His Spirit already. All we have to do is to acknowledge His presence, learn to listen to Him, and then give Him the freedom to operate.

IT'S *WHO* YOU KNOW THAT MATTERS

Then Barnabas went to Tarsus to look for Saul, and when he found him, he brought him to Antioch. So for a whole year Barnabas and Saul met with the church and taught great numbers of people. The disciples were first called Christians at Antioch.

Acts 11:25-26

There was no rhyme or reason for choosing the name 'Cliff Richard'. 'Harry Webb' sounded dreary so a group of us sat round a table and threw names at each other until we arrived eventually at Cliff Richards. I thought 'Richard', without the 's', would make it a bit more noteworthy, so that was that.

I don't imagine there was any careful discussion about the nickname given to Jesus' disciples. It was obvious that they were connected to Christ, so what better than 'Christian'? That's what 'ian' at the end of a word means — 'connected to'. A politician is someone connected to politics, a librarian is connected to libraries and books, and so on. It's a helpful explanation of a Christian too — someone connected to Christ. It still has to be spelt out to some folk that you aren't necessarily a Christian because you were born in Britain, or because you go to church, or because you've been christened or confirmed, or even because you're kind to your neighbour. You're a Christian only if you're connected to Jesus, and that means if, by faith, you've accepted Him into your life as Saviour, and if you're obeying Him day by day as Lord.

To do well in show-business, like many other professions, connections are important. It isn't what you know that matters, but who you know. That may be an exaggeration in business, but it's spot on for the Christian life. It isn't what you know. No amount of head knowledge or theory, no matter how useful, will give you the right to be nicknamed 'Christian'. It's who you know. The Jesus connection is what matters. If you know Him, you own the name. Be proud of it.

NO COMPARISON

In the past God spoke to our fore-fathers through the prophets at many times and in various ways, but in these last days he has spoken to us by his Son, whom he appointed heir of all things, and through whom he made the universe. The Son is the radiance of God's glory and the exact re-presentation of his being, sustaining all things by his powerful word. After he had provided purification for sins, he sat down at the right hand of the Majesty in heaven. So he became as much superior to the angels as the name he has inherited is superior to theirs.

For to which of the angels did God ever say,
'You are my Son;
today I have become your Father'?
Or again,
'I will be his Father,
and he will be my Son'?
And again, when God brings his firstborn into the world, he says,
'Let all God's angels worship him.'

Hebrews 1:1-6

It would take an expert theologian to shed light on all of this but one thing here is plain and simple — Jesus was no ordinary man. Obvious maybe, but that's what many people think He was — a great leader and teacher but, in the end, just another man, like the eastern guru that the Beatles chased in the Sixties, or like any one of a thousand and one outstanding, powerful people who have attracted followers down the centuries. If Jesus were just another great man, then it follows that Christianity would be just another man-made philosophy and, goodness knows, there are scores of those, old and new, some good, some worthless. You pays your money and takes your choice.

But Jesus was more than that. His uniqueness sets Christianity apart from all other doctrines and beliefs and convinces me that this is Truth. Who Jesus was is therefore crucial to our faith, and it's why the writer to the Hebrews begins his book by carefully explaining Jesus' real nature.

As I say, I can't grasp it all, but I do appreciate that God and Jesus had a unique relationship, that Jesus was with God from the very beginning of creation, and that He came to earth to reveal just what God is like. Jesus says that when I listen to Him and examine His character, I'm hearing and understanding God Himself. No other man dares claim that, and today Jesus, God's only Son, is with His Father in heaven, more important than any angel, and with His Father's authority and majesty. Beyond that I can't comprehend, but then one day I'll meet Him and it'll all be much clearer!

A QUESTION OF PRIORITIES

Do not store up for yourselves trea-
sures on earth, where moth and rust
destroy, and where thieves break in
and steal. But store up for yourselves
treasures in heaven, where moth and
rust do not destroy, and where thieves
do not break in and steal. For where
your treasure is, there your heart will
be also.

Matthew 6:19-21

I guess even the poorest of people have treasures. They needn't be flashy diamonds or wads of money hidden under the floorboards. They don't have to be smooth cars or country mansions — although things like that certainly figure high in many folk's ambitions. Surprisingly, our treasure could be our weekly pocket money, favourite sport, even a boy or girl friend. Things that in themselves are not bad — far from it — but which can easily become our very top and most time-consuming priority. And that's what I think Jesus is telling us here. It's vital that we get our priorities straight. Money, houses, cars, furniture, hobbies, relationships, jobs — all of those things are part of life. And the Lord gives us all things 'richly to enjoy'. But, do you see, if that's where our heart is — if that's our treasure — then it means that Jesus doesn't have first place, and that's the only position in our lives that He will accept.

Like everything else in the Bible, it's such good sense. If we do set our heart on our bank account, on our record collection, on a pop singer, then literally overnight our dreams and our treasure can be wiped out. Robbery, fire, accident, redundancy, some unexpected change of circumstances and our treasure has gone, and all that's left is a broken and very lonely heart. Compare that to Jesus, who is the same yesterday, today and for ever, and who says there's nothing in this world or out of it that can separate us from His love, who says He'll never forsake us, come what may.

My test came fairly early on in my Christian life when I had to decide just what was more important — my career or my faith. I wrote about it in my book *Which One's Cliff?* and called the chapter 'My Little Isaac'. You see, I love my job. Going on stage before a few thousand people or creating sounds in a recording studio is no hardship. I honestly love it. But I had to consider whether I should give it up if I could serve the Lord better elsewhere. When I'd already made the decision to quit, God showed me clearly that I should stay put. The result of that little experience is that today I know for sure which is more important. In fact I'm more enthusiastic about my career than ever — but I know where my treasure is!

AN OFFER YOU *CAN* REFUSE

Now there is in Jerusalem near the Sheep Gate a pool, which in Aramaic is called Bethesda and which is surrounded by five covered colonnades. Here a great number of disabled people used to lie — the blind, the lame, the paralysed. One who was there had been an invalid for thirty-eight years. When Jesus saw him lying there and learned that he had been in this condition for a long time, he asked him, 'Do you want to get well?'

'Sir,' the invalid replied, 'I have no-one to help me into the pool when the water is stirred. While I am trying to get in, someone else goes down ahead of me.'

Then Jesus said to him, 'Get up! Pick up your mat and walk.' At once the man was cured; he picked up his mat and walked.

John 5:2-9

What a strange question to ask. 'Do you want to get well?' It must have been pretty obvious, surely, or why should the guy have been there? But wait a minute! I remember hearing a story from a missionary in India about a crippled beggar who, day after day, sat at the same spot, hoping for the odd coin from a passer-by. A Christian doctor befriended him and believed that, with surgery, the man's twisted leg could be straightened. The beggar agreed and the operation was successful. For the first time, the man could stand on two feet and move about without assistance.

Some months later, the doctor was shocked to see the same man back at his old spot, begging as before, with his mended leg tucked under him. As the doctor approached, the beggar scowled and looked away. The message was clear. This was the way of life the man preferred. Although a new and better way was now a practical option, he didn't want it. This was what he was used to; this was how he'd stay.

And that's just how this crippled man at the pool may have been thinking. Jesus needed to know that he genuinely wanted to be made well and was prepared to face up to a new lifestyle, with new responsibilities and priorities. Jesus never forced His attention or His help on people who didn't want it. And that's how it still is.

Why don't more people around us respond to Jesus and become Christians once they know about Him? Principally because they simply don't want to. They prefer to cling to the life they know — away from God's demands and God's control — rather than the one on offer from Jesus, despite the promise of new resources and new prospects. Some would say that's shortsighted, but Jesus always insists on giving us the choice. 'Do you want to be made well?'

'I DO IT FOR JESUS'

'Then the King will say to those on his right, "Come, you who are blessed by my Father; take your inheritance, the kingdom prepared for you since the creation of the world. For I was hungry and you gave me something to eat, I was thirsty and you gave me something to drink, I was a stranger and you invited me in, I needed clothes and you clothed me, I was sick and you looked after me, I was in prison and you came to visit me."

'Then the righteous will answer him, "Lord, when did we see you hungry and feed you, or thirsty and give you something to drink? When did we see you a stranger and invite you in, or needing clothes and clothe you? When did we see you sick or in prison and go to visit you?"

'The King will reply, "I tell you the truth, whatever you did for one of the least of these brothers of mine, you did for me."'

Matthew 25:34-40

Some teaching in the Bible leaves room for different interpretations. This is one of those sections that doesn't. What it means is as plain as the nose on your face — if we're Christians, then there has to be practical evidence of it by the way we care for the sick, the poor and the persecuted. Jesus really lays it on the line and, if you read further on in the chapter, His words become sterner. If we neglect to care, then it's as though we neglect Jesus Himself and deny all that our faith stands for.

One of my most sharp-edged memories of visiting India with Tear Fund was being with Mother Teresa in her Home for the Destitute and Dying in Calcutta. The place isn't as terrible as it sounds. The building is simple and clean, and the patients lie peacefully and with dignity on their mattresses. In one place a sister prepares an old emaciated man for death. In another a helper raises a bowl of soup to the lips of a woman too weak to feed herself. Mother Teresa is love personified. 'I do it for Jesus,' she says simply. 'Here is Jesus' — and she points to a beggar who was brought in from the streets. 'And here... and here... and here.' And each time her hand directs me to a child dying of malnutrition, to an old woman who for too long has existed as one of the city's pavement statistics, and to another child who is smiling and wide-eyed yet with a parchment-like face.

I'll never forget her example. 'I do it for Jesus.'

It isn't so easy in Britain. The poor and the hungry and the sick are seldom on our doorsteps as they are, quite literally, in Calcutta, but I doubt if that

excuses us. What kind of 'head in the sand' act are we playing if we plead 'out of sight, out of mind'? Two-thirds of our world live in conditions every bit as bad as Jesus described nearly two thousand years ago, and modern communications have brought them to our attention and to within our reach. Not all of us can be Mother Teresa, but all of us are called to show tangible, practical care in some form or another.

Your local Social Services office would probably suggest some ways, and, for help overseas, there's always Tear Fund who will inform and advise.

N.B. Tear Fund's address is: 11 Station Road, Teddington, Middlesex, TW11 9AA (telephone: 01 977 9144).

A ROCK AND A FORTRESS

*My soul finds rest in God
alone;
my salvation comes from
him.
He alone is my rock and my
salvation;
he is my fortress, I shall
never be shaken.
How long will you assault a
man?
Would all of you throw him
down —
this leaning wall, this
tottering fence?
They fully intend to topple
him
from his lofty place;
they take delight in lies.*

*With their mouths they bless,
but in their hearts they
curse.
Find rest, O my soul, in God
alone;
my hope comes from him.
He alone is my rock and my
salvation;
he is my fortress, I shall not
be shaken.
My salvation and my honour
depend on God,
he is my mighty rock, my
refuge.
Trust in him at all times, O
people;
pour out your hearts to him,
for God is our refuge.*

Psalm 62:1-8

Some parts of the Bible are really quite difficult to understand and there are whole chunks which I still find baffling, even after eighteen years of reading! However, that's no reason at all for skipping the difficult bits, because I'm quite sure that gradually God shows us more and more as we grow up as Christians.

This Psalm is one of those less obvious parts — I suppose because it isn't a straight-forward story. In fact it isn't a story at all — just someone sharing his own experience of God. But if you really study it hard and simply ask the question 'What one thing is God trying to teach me?' then I reckon you will see why I have chosen it.

As far as I am concerned, Psalm 62 — which originally of course was written as a song — reminds me that God is absolutely reliable. Rocks and fortresses can be hammered and bombarded by the toughest waves or enemies, but afterwards they are as solid and dependable as ever. That's how God is — a tower of strength, who can support us when we are weak and tottering.

LEARNING TO LEAN

Let love and faithfulness never leave
   you;
   bind them around your neck,
      write them on the tablet of your
   heart.
Then you will win favour and a good
   name
      in the sight of God and man.
Trust in the LORD with all your heart.
   and lean not on your own
understanding;
   in all your ways acknowledge him.
      and he will make your paths
   straight.
Do not be wise in your own eyes;
   fear the LORD and shun evil.
This will bring health to your body
   and nourishment to your bones.

Proverbs 3:3-8

'Trusting in the Lord' is a beautiful idea but, in my experience, not an easy or an automatic thing to do. Although there may be some who can exercise perfect trust overnight, so to speak, I suspect that, for most Christians, real dependence grows over a period of time and is only genuinely proved and prompted when we are at the end of our own self-sufficiency. Like me, I'm sure you've heard other Christians say that it took a spell of real hardship, illness or whatever, actually to force them to put trust into practice. Usually of course we don't need to trust because we reckon we can cope O.K. with our own resources. When those resources run out, then we realise that 'trusting in the Lord' isn't mere religious jargon or theory. It's something we actually do. And what a fantastic discovery it is when we see that trust in Jesus is neither misplaced nor moronic. The more we trust, says this section of Proverbs, and the less we rely on our own natural wisdom, the more we'll discover that God is involved in and leading our lives.

God's guidance can be a tortuous thing to unravel. I must confess that I've never had to agonise over a major decision, desperately trying to find the mind of the Lord in the matter. Whereas there's no doubt that God does sometimes make His path clear via the advice of others, circumstances, conscience and so on, I think that just as often we have to use our God-given common-sense and make a decision, believing that we are sufficiently in tune with God's Spirit that our conclusion will be the right one. If it isn't then, as sure as anything, we'll know it before long.

NO DEBTS

Now Eli, who was very old, heard about everything his sons were doing to all Israel and how they slept with the women who served at the entrance to the Tent of Meeting. So he said to them, 'Why do you do such things? I hear from all the people about these wicked deeds of yours. No, my sons; it is not a good report that I hear spreading among the LORD'S people. If a man sins against another man, God may mediate for him; but if a man sins against the LORD, who will intercede for him?' His sons, however, did not listen to their father's rebuke, for it was the LORD'S will to put them to death.

'Therefore the LORD, the God of Israel, declares: "I promised that your house and your father's house would minister before me for ever." But now the LORD declares: "Far be it from me! Those who honour me I will honour, but those who despise me will be disdained."'

1 Samuel 2:22-25, 30

What a fantastic film 'Chariots of Fire' was! I wonder if you saw it? One of the main characters was Eric Liddell, an athlete and a Christian, who lived earlier this century. The film was partly about Eric's rise to fame as an international runner, and the pressures brought on him to compromise what he believed. It was brought to a head when the preliminary heats of the Olympic Games were scheduled for a Sunday. Eric was due to compete in those heats, but Sunday was the Sabbath and to run in any race would be in direct conflict with the Bible's teaching as he understood it. What should he do? Was it more important to represent his country, or to be obedient to God? Despite heavy persuasion to compete, Eric was in no doubt. God was the number one priority in his life, and he would pull out of the race.

No sooner had he announced his decision, to the dismay of the Olympic Committee, than there was a solution. Eric would take the place of a fellow athlete in an alternative race, scheduled for another day. It was a race in which his arch-rival, a world record holder from America, was also competing. A moment before the starter's signal, when every eye in the French stadium was riveted to the track, a message was passed to Eric on a scrap of paper. It was from Scholz, one of the stars of the American team. It said simply: 'He who honours me, I also will honour'.

Eric won his race, and years later went to China as a missionary.

God, says the Bible, is no man's debtor.

START ALL OVER AGAIN

Now there was a man of the Pharisees named Nicodemus, a member of the Jewish ruling council. He came to Jesus at night and said, 'Rabbi, we know you are a teacher who has come from God. For no-one could perform the miraculous signs you are doing if God were not with him.'

In reply Jesus declared, 'I tell you the truth, unless a man is born again, he cannot see the kingdom of God.'

'How can a man be born when he is old?' Nicodemus asked. 'Surely he cannot enter a second time into his mother's womb to be born!'

Jesus answered, 'I tell you the truth, unless a man is born of water and the Spirit, he cannot enter the kingdom of God. Flesh gives birth to flesh, but the Spirit gives birth to spirit. You should not be surprised at my saying, "You must be born again."'

John 3:1-7

'Are you an ordinary Christian,' a reporter asked me recently, 'or one of those new-fangled "born again" ones?' I understood the question, but groaned at the thought of yet more misunderstanding creeping in about what a Christian really is. The phrase 'born again' is hardly 'new-fangled', considering Jesus used it, nor does it denote any new 'super breed' of Christian, more pious and religious than the rest.

Let's be clear that being 'born again' doesn't describe any category of Christian — there are no such things as categories. A person is either a Christian or not a Christian, and that's the end of it. What it does describe is the process of becoming a Christian which, according to Jesus, is common to *everyone* who becomes part of God's family, and experiences, consciously or subconsciously, a new beginning.

When we're born, it's the start of our physical life; when we become Christians, it's the start of our spiritual life. We're born again — for a second time. Nicodemus needed it spelt out to him. No, Jesus explained, He didn't mean that a person had to go back to his mother's womb (I wonder if Nicodemus was deliberately being a bit thick), but the second birth was another kind of miracle, brought about by God's Spirit, and was just as creative.

To make it personal, when I became a Christian, the spiritual dimension of my life, which had lain dormant for twenty-four years, woke up. Suddenly this whole new area of awareness and interest burst into life and I became a more complete person, a brand-new baby Christian, who needed feeding and nurturing.

So don't be confused. God has no brand names. The question is not what kind of Christian you are, but whether you're a Christian at all; whether you've been born again into a new family.

LIKE A LAMB TO THE SLAUGHTER

Surely he took up our
infirmities
and carried our sorrows,
yet we considered him stricken
by God,
smitten by him, and
afflicted.
But he was pierced for our
transgressions,
he was crushed for our iniquities;
the punishment that brought
us peace was upon him,
and by his wounds we are healed.

We all, like sheep, have gone astray,
each of us has turned to his own
way;
and the LORD has laid on him the
iniquity of us all.
He was oppressed and afflicted,
yet he did not open his mouth;
he was led like a lamb to the
slaughter,
and as a sheep before her shearers
is silent,
so he did not open his mouth.

Isaiah 53:4-7

What a beautiful part of the Bible this is, and I don't mind admitting that tears come to my eyes when I read it. It's remarkable of course that Isaiah should have been able to predict what happened to Jesus so long before He came to earth, and this is one of those Old Testament prophecies that gives the whole Bible God's stamp of authority and binds Old and New Testaments into a single entity.

But come on, read this section again, and tell me if you aren't moved. The picture of Jesus going to His death like a lamb to the slaughter, innocent and unprotesting, and going in my place, taking my punishment, just has to evoke a response. Emotional it may be, but so what? Emotions are part of our make-up and, as long as our minds function at the same time, we mustn't discount them. The crucifixion of Jesus is an emotional story, but don't let's veer away from the implications of it simply because we're frightened of our emotions. In my book, it's not unmanly to weep when circumstances warrant it.

Jesus was wounded, bruised, chastised, beaten, oppressed and afflicted so that you and I can be healed and made whole. And people ask what I find exciting about Christianity! If that isn't the most dynamic good news for a seemingly lost and hopeless world, I don't know what is.

FRIEND IN HIGH PLACES

My command is this: Love each other as I have loved you. Greater love has no-one than this, that one lay down his life for his friends. You are my friends if you do what I command. I no longer call you servants, because a servant does not know his master's business. Instead, I have called you friends, for everything that I learned from my Father I have made known to you. You did not choose me, but I chose you to go and bear fruit — fruit that will last. Then the Father will give you whatever you ask in my name. This is my command: Love each other.

John 15:12-17

Imagine someone telling you he was the friend of the Queen. You'd think he was either pulling your leg or had a screw loose. But suppose he was telling the truth and really knew the Royal Family and spent time with them regularly? You'd quickly change your opinion and recognise that this had to be someone special. To have met the Queen is one thing; to actually be her friend is another — a privilege reserved for only a few.

Do you realise that every Christian can claim, with total confidence, to be a friend of the King — not a servant or a slave, but a friend, God's friend? And it's God who has chosen us for the privilege. I know it's extraordinary but that's what Jesus said and you won't find me arguing. I certainly don't deserve it. I've been a pretty miserable friend in return — but that alters nothing. The fact is that the King of all Kings and the Lord of all Lords, the Creator of the universe (about which man knows only a tiny fraction) has chosen you and me to be His friends.

Forget that old nonsense about God being some stern headmaster figure whose main concern is to punish and rap us over the knuckles, or that He is some remote impersonal force *à la* 'Star Wars'. That's not the God of the Bible. For sure, He wants us to follow in his way but, for the God who calls me friend, that's the least I can do.

PLAIN MIND-BOGGLING

O LORD, our Lord,
how majestic is your name
in all the earth!

You have set your glory
above the heavens.
From the lips of children and
infants
you have ordained praise
because of your enemies,
to silence the foe and the
avenger.

When I consider your
heavens,
the work of your fingers,

the moon and the stars,
which you have set in place,
what is man that you are
mindful of him,
the son of man that you
care for him?

You made him a little lower
than the heavenly beings
and crowned him with glory
and honour.

Psalm 8:1-5

It's funny how every so often something you read sticks in your mind. This little item must have been in a school textbook — so it's six or seven years now since I saw it! Dealing with astronomy and the various planets and galaxies, the book mentioned that there were more stars in the universe than all the grains of sand on all the beaches in the world. I remember my mind boggling to comprehend that at the time and, to be honest, I still find it hard to accept — it's just too big a concept. Yet it's beyond dispute. There are too many stars ever to be counted. Just billion upon billion, endless, and the most powerful of our telescopes can only scratch at the vastness. All our space discovery, exploration and expertise put together must represent a pinpoint on a football, and the more our scientists learn, the more we realise how puny our knowledge is.

And behind this incomprehensibly complex universe is a Creator. That's not hard to believe. It would take more faith than I can find to believe there was no design, only random chance. I've yet to meet a genuine atheist. The ones who tell me they don't believe there's a God invariably turn out to be regular agnostics — they don't really know. When eventually I meet someone who's convinced there's no God, no Creator, I'll disagree with his views but admire his faith.

As I say, I have no problem believing in a Creator. The extraordinary aspect of Christian belief is that this great, all-powerful Creator God, who holds the whole universe together, is aware of insignificant ants like us. And not only does He know about me and about you — He loves us and longs to have our love in return. It *is* mind-boggling — far-fetched even. If it weren't for Jesus bridging the gulf, it would be almost too good to be true.

ALL MY LOVE

No-one has ever gone into heaven except the one who came from heaven — the Son of Man. Just as Moses lifted up the snake in the desert, so the Son of Man must be lifted up, that everyone who believes may have eternal life in him.

For God so loved the world that he gave his one and only Son, that whoever believes in him shall not perish but have eternal life. For God did not send his Son into the world to condemn the world, but to save the world through him.

John 3:13-17

There's no doubt that, if this is true — particularly the bit about God loving the world, I mean — then it has to be the most radical, urgent and relevant piece of good news ever to be delivered. Personally, I am as convinced about the truth of it as I am about anything. When I first began to grasp the implications, many of my attitudes and priorities had to be revised, and in fact my whole life took on quite a change of direction!

I know it's a concept that's hard to handle, but put it, first of all, in personal terms, and simply be open to the possibility that God really does love you so much that He gave Jesus to die so that you need not fear or experience the consequences of death yourself.

Of course, that's the very heart of the Christian gospel, far removed from sombre suits or musty buildings. I think it was Billy Graham who was asked what he would say if he had just sixty seconds to address a crowd. 'I'd simply read John 3:16,' said Dr Graham. 'It's all a person needs to know.'

In my post-bag I receive a lot of sad letters from lonely people. Often the problems are basic: they feel unloved and unimportant, and nobody cares. Often I get a friend to reply and explain very firmly that that just isn't true, and, if only they could wrap themselves in the security of God's love, then life would take on a whole new perspective. The point is that we *are* valuable, each one of us, and when we wake up to that truth we start to realise the worth of our neighbour as well.

Just close your mind to everything else then, and chew over the words again. 'For God so loved the world . . .'

And, in case you think it's all a bit abstract and academic, remember that what you believe has to be lived!

FIT TO BURST

When they saw the courage of Peter and John and realised that they were unschooled, ordinary men, they were astonished and they took note that these men had been with Jesus. But since they could see the man who had been healed standing there with them, there was nothing they could say. So they ordered them to withdraw from the Sanhedrin and then conferred together.

Then they called them in again and commanded them not to speak or teach at all in the name of Jesus. But Peter and John replied, 'Judge for yourselves whether it is right in God's sight to obey you rather than God. For we cannot help speaking about what we have seen and heard.'

Acts 4:13-15, 18-20

Those early Christians didn't pull any punches. The impact they had on society was powerful and startling, and for some, like the religious ruling authority, the Sanhedrin, it was downright embarrassing. Peter and John had been arrested after a cripple had been miraculously healed, and hauled before the Jewish leaders. Already word was spreading fast about Jesus being alive and that it was through His power that miracles were taking place and lives were being changed. It was worrying for the Sanhedrin. Something had to be done. These Christ-followers and their teaching had to be stamped out. They were too much of a threat.

Two things I love about this story. The first is that Peter and John were simple ordinary men. Not an O-level between them, and that bothered the Sanhedrin. If the prisoners had been scholars, trained in oratory or politics, it would have been more understandable, but Peter and John were common fishermen. How did they have the ability, let alone the nerve, to stand in front of such an important and powerful council and argue their case? Ignorant men such as these should cringe and cower, not speak with authority and confidence.

Of course the Sanhedrin knew their secret, although I suspect they never realised it. 'They took note,' it says, 'that these men had been with Jesus.' That was the reason for their courage. They had been affected by Jesus, and it's been like that all through the centuries. When people spend time with Jesus, getting to know Him, they can't help but be different. Sometimes today I meet people who I remember as timid and aimless, who, because they have 'been with Jesus' and have been changed by Him, are now sure of where they're going and are totally unashamed to give all the credit to Him.

And that's the second ingredient of this story that's significant for me. When Peter and John were warned in no uncertain terms to keep their mouths shut and never to speak of Jesus again, their answer was crisp and to the point. 'Is it more important to obey you or God?' they asked — and I can imagine the pompous Sanhedrin members growing purple with rage. How could they reply? The answer was obvious. 'As far as we are concerned,' the two apostles added, 'we can't help ourselves. We have to speak about what we've seen and heard.'

That was a fantastic statement and it's the precise reason why I and every other committed Christian have to talk about our faith in Jesus. It's the experience of Him in our lives that we want to share. Not theory about Him from a textbook; Christianity is no second-hand religion. Its essence is what we've seen and heard, and that should make us as eager to tell it as Peter and John were.

WHEN JESUS DIED

At the sixth hour darkness came over the whole land until the ninth hour. And at the ninth hour Jesus cried out in a loud voice, 'Eloi, Eloi, lama sabachthani?' — which means, 'My God, my God, why have you forsaken me?'

With a loud cry, Jesus breathed his last.
The curtain of the temple was torn in two from top to bottom. And when the centurion, who stood there in front of Jesus, heard his cry and saw how he died, he said, 'Surely this man was the Son of God!'

Mark 15:33-34, 37-39

There's no way we can really identify with the depth of Jesus' suffering when He was hanging on the cross. The physical agony of it all was appalling enough, and I'm sure you know the details of Roman crucifixion as well as I do. Think of hanging by your arms in the gym, with your back to the wall bars, for hours on end, and you'll have a tiny hint of just the strain alone. But the physical torture was only part of Jesus' suffering, and it wasn't the pain of His body that caused Him to cry out, 'My God! My God! Why have you forsaken me?' For the first time ever, Jesus knew what it was like to be absolutely alone. At the moment when He needed comfort and spiritual resources as never before, Father and Son were separated, and I guess that no human finite mind can quite understand the profound spiritual loneliness and despair that caused.

If we understand why the separation occurred, why God deserted His son at that critical time, then we'll understand the very heart of the Christian faith, and why it's often said that Christianity starts at the cross. Paul explains it simply in his letter to the Corinthians: 'God made Jesus, who had no sin, to be sin for us'.

In other words, during those extraordinary minutes of history, Jesus, who had no sin of His own and could therefore be absolutely at one and in harmony with His Father, took on the sin of the whole of humanity. Your sin and mine,

everything that spoils and drags us down, was nailed there with Jesus. Now do you see why God turned away? He could have no association or relationship with anything that was less than perfect. Throughout the Old Testament we're taught that God is pure and holy and demands that His people should be pure and holy too. When they failed, it had to be a perfect lamb that was sacrificed on their behalf. Nothing impure, nothing spoiled, nothing less than perfection would be acceptable. It's no wonder that, for those moments, Jesus must have been abhorrent to His Father.

Forget the world's sin. That's too huge a concept to comprehend. Just imagine Jesus dealing with yours. That would have been cause enough for God to turn away and for Jesus to experience His isolation.

I'm no theologian and couldn't begin to answer all the questions about what happened at Calvary, but I know myself, and I know what I deserve from a God who is perfect and demands perfection. I'm only grateful, and want my life to be a 'thank you' to the God who now accepts me as perfect because Jesus wiped the slate clean when He became 'my sin' on the cross.

If you've only thought of the crucifixion as a sentimental story, an excuse for a Good Friday holiday, please think again. There's so much more.

CAN'T TAKE THE HURT ANY MORE

Then seizing him, they led him away and took him into the house of the high priest. Peter followed at a distance. But when they had kindled a fire in the middle of the courtyard and had sat down together, Peter sat down with them.

A servant girl saw him seated there in the firelight. She looked closely at him and said, 'This man was with him.'

But he denied it. 'Woman, I don't know him,' he said.

A little later someone else saw him and said, 'You also are one of them.'

'Man, I am not!' Peter replied.

About an hour later another asserted, 'Certainly this fellow was with him, for he is a Galilean.'

Peter replied, 'Man, I don't know what you're talking about!' Just as he was speaking, the cock crowed. The Lord turned and looked straight at Peter. Then Peter remembered the word the Lord had spoken to him: 'Before the cock crows today, you will disown me three times.' And he went outside and wept bitterly.

Luke 22:54-62

'Never let your heart rule your head,' goes the old saying. Well, mine does, often, so I relate easily to Peter, who had the same problem. A few hours before, he was confident and determined. 'Lord,' he had said, 'I'm ready to go with you to prison and to death.' Good old Peter! I'm sure he meant it at the time and couldn't understand why Jesus wasn't so optimistic. But Jesus knew Peter better than he knew himself. In a crowd of like-minded people, with Jesus up front, Peter was in fighting mood. He was ready to take on the world. There was no way he'd let Jesus down. The idea was unthinkable.

What a difference a few hours can make. Jesus had been arrested and led away, the other disciples had vanished into the night, and Peter was alone. The security of Jesus and his friends was suddenly stripped away and he was vulnerable and weak. He looked around for moral support but there was no sign of any. The atmosphere was hostile and, for the first time in nearly three years, Peter, nicknamed 'The Rock' — the first always to volunteer — was afraid and couldn't even face a servant girl with the truth.

There must have been millions of parallels since then. People buoyed up by the emotion of some Christian meeting or rally, determined to give their right arm for Jesus, only to be ashamed of Him and deny any connection at work the next day. Like Peter, we're so easily afraid. Afraid of what other people will think, afraid of being embarrassed or misunderstood, afraid of being unpopular or made to look silly. At least Peter's fear was of genuine physical danger. Ours is usually of social nonconformity.

If the story ended with Peter in tears, there wouldn't be much encouragement for us. The fact is that, in the book of Acts, he emerges as one of the most courageous and outstanding of early Christians, and it seems likely that, because of his refusal to compromise or be silent about his faith in Jesus, he was killed upside-down on a Roman cross.

What caused the change? How did that lonely, demoralised disciple in the courtyard become Peter, the fearless apostle? There's only one answer - the Holy Spirit, God's presence arriving in Peter's life to effect the change. There's no other explanation for his new character, new resources and new gifts.

From the evidence I see around me, the Holy Spirit is still at work in no less a dramatic and powerful way. I see Him changing the lives of friends and bringing strength and vitality and enthusiasm into situations which were dull and lifeless. Many churches around the world are waking up and discovering that the Holy Spirit isn't locked away in the New Testament but is as real and available and as potent a force today as He was to Peter all those centuries ago.

Dig around the church scene and discover for yourself what's happening. You'll be amazed!

MOSES' POWERHOUSE

The Amalekites came and attacked the Israelites at Rephidim. Moses said to Joshua, 'Choose some of our men and go out to fight the Amalekites. Tomorrow I will stand on top of the hill with the staff of God in my hands.'

So Joshua fought the Amalekites as Moses had ordered, and Moses, Aaron and Hur went to the top of the hill. As long as Moses held up his hands, the Israelites were winning. When Moses' hands grew tired, they took a stone and put it under him and he sat on it. Aaron and Hur held his hands up — one on one side, one on the other — so that his hands remained steady till sunset. So Joshua overcame the Amalekite army with the sword.

Exodus 17:8-13

What an odd sight that must have been. Moses, old and frail, praying to God on the top of a hill, with someone either side to support his outstretched arms, while down below a full-scale battle was being fought. In those days, people didn't pray with heads bowed and eyes closed. It was head back, eyes looking to the skies, and arms held high. So, when Moses prayed, the battle went well; when he tired and stopped, the enemy gained the upper hand.

There would have been some in that Jewish army who would have written Moses off. He was too old, too doddery, to be of any use. For others, who knew better, the sight of Moses at prayer must have instilled new heart and confidence. They knew from past experience that, when Moses prayed, the Lord answered, and this occasion was no different. The battle was won because Moses knew he had to pray. That was his responsibility and, even though he was physically weak and needed support, he gritted his teeth and prayed on — arms in the air, head up, eyes open.

Do you know the one thing that Christian missionaries overseas request more than anything else from folk at home? It's prayer. 'Tell the people to pray for us,' was the message I was given time and time again when I visited Christian workers in Bangladesh and India. Financial support is necessary, letters are an encouragement, but prayer is the lifeline. 'I could never have gone on if it weren't for the prayers of people back home', said one nurse. 'Prayer is like a powerhouse. Switch it off and you're useless. Turn it on and there's an energy let loose which makes nothing impossible.'

What a blessing are those really dedicated praying Christians — many of them old folk who are confined to their houses maybe, yet spend literally hour after hour praying for people and situations that God puts in their minds and on their hearts. I know I shall never meet a fraction of the people who pray for me regularly, but I'm grateful for them and for the spiritual resources they seem to unlock.

Prayer is another of those mysteries that you can't analyse or reduce to a formula. But don't underestimate it. James wrote in his New Testament letter: 'The prayer of a righteous man is powerful and effective.' Put it to the test.

TAKING NO CHANCES!

While Paul was waiting for them in Athens, he was greatly distressed to see that the city was full of idols.

Then they took him and brought him to a meeting of the Areopagus, where they said to him, 'May we know what this new teaching is that you are presenting? You are bringing some strange ideas to our ears, and we want to know what they mean.'

(All the Athenians and the foreigners who lived there spent their time doing nothing but talking about and listening to the latest ideas.)

Paul then stood up in the meeting of the Areopagus and said: 'Men of Athens! I see that in every way you are very religious. For as I walked round and observed your objects of worship, I even found an altar with this inscription: TO AN UNKNOWN GOD. Now what you worship as something unknown I am going to proclaim to you.'

Acts 17:16, 19-23

Hang on a minute before you wipe out the Athenians too critically. There's little doubt that they were a superstitious lot, with altars and statues all over the place to every imaginable god. It's as if they were hedging their bets: 'Better not leave anyone out just in case!' For good measure and to leave no loophole, they even had an altar to 'The Unknown God'.

I say don't be too critical because I'm not sure that our society is all that much better. For a start, we worship all manner of gods — more subtle than the Greeks had and admittedly less 'religious', but gods all the same. I'm thinking of houses, for instance; cars, money, sport, television and — I'm the first to admit it — pop music and pop stars. In other words, things that claim top priority and top allegiance in our lives, and which are often lumped together under the general heading of 'materialism'. God has been elbowed out by 'things'.

And the similarity goes further. If there were a Gallup Poll to discover attitudes to God, I suspect the majority opinion would be 'I don't know'. All of us, I'm sure, have a deep-down instinct to believe in someone outside of ourselves. The fact that, according to the Bible, we're created 'in God's image' confirms that. But instinct is easily submerged and we're content to allow our belief to stagnate at the level of the 'Star Wars' 'Force'. Someone, somewhere probably, but impersonal, unknowable and not much to do with living and working in the 1980s.

Perhaps there was more excuse for the Athenians. They had little opportunity to find out about their 'unknown God' until Paul came along and spelt it out. They certainly learned about Him then. We, on the other hand, have had the best part of 2,000 years of Christian history, as well as a complete Bible to study. We have hundreds of Christian teachers, thousands of helpful books, cassettes and now video tapes — all communicating to society truth about the God who longs to be known and to receive our love.

The problem perhaps is that we're not that keen to find out.

YES, HE LIVES

But if it is preached that Christ has been raised from the dead, how can some of you say that there is no resurrection of the dead? If there is no resurrection of the dead, then not even Christ has been raised. And if Christ has not been raised, our preaching is useless and so is your faith. More than that, we are then found to be false witnesses about God, for we have testified about God that he raised Christ from the dead. But he did not raise him if in fact the dead are not raised. For if the dead are not raised, then Christ has not been raised either. And if Christ has not been raised, your faith is futile; you are still in your sins. Then those also who have fallen asleep in Christ are lost. If only for this life we have hope in Christ, we are to be pitied more than all men.

1 Corinthians 15:12-19

A favourite story of mine is about the lawyer who set out, logically and rationally, to debunk Christianity by disproving the Resurrection. He knew that, if he could show that Jesus had stayed in that tomb, Christians would have the heart torn from their faith. Instead of a risen, living Jesus, still active in the world and in His people, all there would be was a memory. Certainly Jesus would remain a great man but that's all. He'd be assured of a place in history but would never have a place in people's lives.

So the lawyer marshalled his facts, researched every possible document and item of evidence, and arrived eventually at his conclusion — but not the one he intended. All the weight of evidence, instead of pouring doubt on Jesus' resurrection, indicated exactly the opposite — that the Bible accounts were accurate and that, three days after execution on a Roman cross, Jesus came back from death.

Do you see why that's so central and why a living contemporary Jesus gives Christianity its uniqueness? Other faiths boast good and wise teachers, many have outstanding leaders who inspire their followers to live disciplined lives, but those men are dead and it's only their words and their memories that live on. They're mortal, just as we are, and I know that no mortal, however sincere, well-meaning or brilliant, can offer me forgiveness and put me right with God. I can't base my life on just the example of a man who lived and died two thousand years ago. There's no way that, however much I admired his teaching, I could actually do what he said. I'm too weak, too prone to failure when it comes to keeping rules. Maybe some can live by philosophies. I know I can't and that's what Paul was meaning. What a miserable, demoralised, frustrated lot Christians would be if it weren't for the fact that Jesus is alive and available, ready and willing to demonstrate His power and vitality in people's lives, if only they'd recognise Him and hand over to Him.

Oh — I nearly forgot — the lawyer did just that. After writing his book — it's called *Who Moved The Stone?* — he became a Christian.

GRUBBY HANDS

I pray for them. I am not praying for the world, but for those you have given me, for they are yours. All I have is yours, and all you have is mine. And glory has come to me through them. I will remain in the world no longer, but they are still in the world, and I am coming to you. Holy Father, protect them by the power of your name — the name you gave me — so that they may be one as we are one. While I was with them, I protected them and kept them safe by that name you gave me. None has been lost except the one doomed to destruction so that Scripture would be fulfilled.

I am coming to you now, but I say these things while I am still in the world, so that they may have the full measure of my joy within them. I have given them your word and the world has hated them, for they are not of the world any more than I am of the world. My prayer is not that you take them out of the world but that you protect them from the evil one. They are not of the world, even as I am not of it. Sanctify them by the truth; your word is truth. As you have sent me into the world, I have sent them into the world. For them I sanctify myself, that they too may be truly sanctified.

John 17:9-19

This is part of a fantastic prayer that Jesus prayed to His Father. Take my advice — just look it up in the Bible and read all of it. It takes up the whole of Chapter 17. Jesus is praying for us — His present-day disciples — and the depth of His concern and love hits you right between the eyes. He knows the pressures of life, and the difficulties and the distractions — all of them — because He went through the whole range of opposition Himself. That's why He can identify so closely and lovingly. He isn't just imagining the tough times; He suffered them personally.

Notice the bit about being 'sent into the world'. I suppose God could have separated His people off to some safe unspoilt corner of the universe. He could have wrapped us in cottonwool and we'd all be one big cosy holy huddle. Comfortable maybe, but not what God intends.

We're to be out getting our hands grubby in the real world. Sure, Christians are different and we're to be conscious of our new family status, but that doesn't mean we're to be in any sense aloof or, heaven forbid, 'holier than thou'. It's often concerned me that, when working people become Christians, they're sometimes advised by other older Christians (who should know better) to leave their job and take on some 'more Christian' occupation. Wrong! Apart from the fact that there are very few jobs which are wholly incompatible with Christian faith (gambling joints and the porn trade would be mighty difficult to reconcile!) our place of work is invariably the most strategic area for sharing our Christian experience. The chances are that Christians will be very thin on the ground in your local office or factory — which is exactly why you should be there and function as God's ambassador.

I see now what a cop-out it would have been if I'd quit show-business, as I nearly did after my conversion. Well-meaning, but maybe timid, Christians said, 'Come out, there are too many pitfalls.' But Jesus prayed about the pitfalls and I trust God to help me avoid them. It's the folk in my industry who need Jesus that I mustn't avoid.

'My prayer isn't that you take them out of the world,' Jesus said, 'but that you protect them from the evil one.' Keep that in mind, when you plan a career — although I realise that you may still have a few more school years to see through first!

AN INCOME POLICY

But godliness with contentment is great gain. For we brought nothing into the world, and we can take nothing out of it. But if we have food and clothing, we will be content with that. People who want to get rich fall into temptation and a trap and into many foolish and harmful desires that plunge men into ruin and destruction. For the love of money is a root of all kinds of evil. Some people, eager for money, have wandered from the faith and pierced themselves with many griefs.

Command those who are rich in this present world not to be arrogant nor to put their hope in wealth, which is so uncertain, but to put their hope in God, who richly provides us with everything for our enjoyment. Command them to do good, to be rich in good deeds, and to be generous and willing to share. In this way they will lay up treasure for themselves as a firm foundation for the coming age, so that they may take hold of the life that is truly life.

1 Timothy 6:6-10, 17-19

Isn't it interesting that the Bible doesn't say that having money is wrong? What it hammers hard is that having a lot of it can be dangerous. I'm fortunate in having a broad spectrum of friends — some rich, some relatively poor — and it's as plain as can be that business success and wealth aren't necessarily a formula for happiness and contentment.

Notice, however, that there's nothing here that condemns ambition. It seems perfectly right that we should use the gifts we have in the best and most responsible way. It's very much a Bible principle that we should be the best at whatever our occupation is. If we're a greengrocer, then let's aim at having the best business in town. If we're at school, then let's not be content with anything less than the best we can give in every subject.

But there's a big difference between healthy ambition and wanting to succeed in order to get rich. If that's our motivation then think again, because we have one foot in the trap already. And, while you're checking that out, what about the great phrase here about God 'who richly provides us with everything for our enjoyment'. God is no killjoy. I suspect He's delighted when we can enjoy a good meal, whether it be eggs, bacon, baked beans and fried bread (one of my favourites) or *boeuf en croute* at the Ritz. They are His gifts, He gave them for our enjoyment — and the same applies to so much more.

Dare I suggest that there are some Christians who ought to start enjoying life a little more? Of course there's much in God's world that's desperately wrong and should tear us apart, but we mustn't get the balance wrong. What you and I have is from God, says the Bible. Most of us have a great deal — and sometimes that warrants a party! So go on, enjoy yourself — but make sure you start enjoying God too.

MENTAL DIETS

Rejoice in the Lord always. I will say it again: Rejoice! Let your gentleness be evident to all. The Lord is near. Do not be anxious about anything, but in everything, by prayer and petition, with thanksgiving, present your requests to God. And the peace of God, which transcends all understanding, will guard your hearts and your minds in Christ Jesus.

Finally, brothers, whatever is true, whatever is noble, whatever is right, whatever is pure, whatever is lovely, whatever is admirable — if anything is excellent or praiseworthy — think about such things. Whatever you have learned or received or heard from me, or seen in me — put it into practice. And the God of peace will be with you.

Philippians 4:4-9

Sometimes I think our society is getting its priorities all topsy-turvy. A review I had once in a national paper is an incredible example. It was after one of my T.V. shows and a critic (obviously not a fan) reported that the programme was 'so wholesome it made me sick'. Now I'd have understood if he had hated the music or the jokes or the format — or all of it put together (some people have no taste!). But the show was panned for being wholesome. A compliment for me, but surely an awful indictment on the writer. Is it really bad to be wholesome? Could he really have been reflecting society — which is getting so accustomed to T.V. violence, cheap morality and lavatory-wall language and humour that anything which doesn't compete on that level is inferior? Surely we can't have slipped that far — but it serves as a nasty warning nevertheless. A constant barrage of the squalid is bound to blur our discernment between right and wrong, good and bad — and if that sounds reminiscent of Mary Whitehouse, I make no apology. I know that if I watch a surfeit of programmes with sub-Christian content, the easier it is for me to think on a sub-Christian level. Insidiously the rubbish we watch and listen to becomes the norm, and even acquires a kind of respectability.

Don't get me wrong. I'm not advocating a diet of 'Gardeners' Question Time', spiced with a little 'Epilogue'. Some Christians have too great a tendency already to cocoon themselves from the real world. Paul set the general principle — that in our watching, reading, listening and talking, we should be focusing on the excellent and the praiseworthy. It's up to us in the Eighties to discern exactly what that is!

MY KINDA LIFE

Therefore Jesus said again, 'I tell you the truth, I am the gate for the sheep. All who ever came before me were thieves and robbers, but the sheep did not listen to them. I am the gate; whoever enters through me will be saved. He will come in and go out, and find pasture. The thief comes only to steal and kill and destroy; I have come that they may have life, and have it to the full.

'I am the good shepherd. The good shepherd lays down his life for the sheep.'

John 10:7-11

All of us, in our different ways, are trying to get the best out of life. Only a fool would opt for Grade B living when there's a Grade A alternative. As I see it, I've only one life to live and I want to live it to the full. Anything less would be a frustration and a waste. The big debate of course centres on how you achieve that maximum. Is it through wealth, job satisfaction, popularity, a secure home, good education? Or is it just an accident of fate and all down to temperament and personality?

Maybe Jesus' words here are intended for those who reckon there's more to life than they've discovered so far. A bit like my conclusion after five or six years in show-business. I was earning a fortune, loving my work, had a happy home, was being screamed at all over the world — yet I knew that there had to be something more. There was some dimension or potential or whatever it was that I was sure hadn't been tapped. And that set me searching and, well, you know the rest.

At the time, I wasn't familiar with Jesus' claim about giving 'life to the full'. As far as I can remember, I shared the popular idea that Christianity was a cramping killjoy religion which prevented you from doing what you really enjoyed and insisted on a dreary narrow lifestyle.

I can only speak from my experience of course, but there's no way that it's been like that. My years as a Christian have been far and away more rewarding than any time before and, instead of narrowing horizons, my interests, contacts and friends have broadened, and priorities have changed and deepened. I'd better add though that the fulness isn't synonymous with ease or permanent happiness. There are aspects of Christian living that are anything but cosy and jolly but, if it's fulfilment you're after, if you have a sense of 'missing out', then consider whether Jesus might not be the key to new and unexplored territory. He offers 'life to the full'. It's an offer you can't ignore.

MUCH MORE VALUABLE

Therefore I tell you, do not worry about your life, what you will eat or drink; or about your body, what you will wear. Is not life more important than food, and the body more important than clothes? Look at the birds of the air; they do not sow or reap or store away in barns, and yet your heavenly Father feeds them. Are you not much more valuable than they? Who of you by worrying can add a single hour to his life?

And why do you worry about clothes? See how the lilies of the field grow. They do not labour or spin. Yet I tell you that not even Solomon in all his splendour was dressed like one of these. If that is how God clothes the grass of the field, which is here today and tomorrow is thrown into the fire, will he not much more clothe you, O you of little faith? So do not worry, saying, 'What shall we eat?' or 'What shall we drink?' or 'What shall we wear?' For the pagans run after all these things, and your heavenly Father knows that you need them. But seek first his kingdom and his righteousness, and all these things will be given to you as well. Therefore do not worry about tomorrow, for tomorrow will worry about itself. Each day has enough trouble of its own.

Matthew 6:25-34

'Not to worry' is easier said than done, I know. But if we really believe that God is Lord and Creator and a loving Father, then it kind of rules out the need to fret and panic about what He must know we have to have anyway. I guess it boils down to simple trust in His provision — often via our ability (which He gave us in the first place!).

But it isn't the worrying that caught my eye when I read this — it's that one little phrase about being 'much more valuable'. Swallow hard and think about it! That you — whoever you are, reading this book — actually matter to God. That, no matter how inadequate, weak, rotten or unimportant you might feel, God regards you as priceless, because He made you and loves you. Now I'm only too well aware that some people, especially in my business, think far too highly of themselves. They think they're the cat's whiskers and the bee's knees rolled into one, and need to be reminded that maybe they're more like the gorilla's armpit! But, strange as it seems, there are many who don't think of themselves highly enough and, as a result, don't think highly about their neighbours either. Remember that commandment about loving our neighbour as much as we love ourselves? Obviously that won't work if we reckon we're so much rubbish.

So, if your self-respect is a bit low, hold your head up — God thinks you're important enough to die for!

I'M THE LONELY ONE

Meanwhile, the older son was in the field. When he came near the house, he heard music and dancing.

So he called one of the servants and asked him what was going on.

'Your brother has come,' he replied, 'and your father has killed the fattened calf because he has him back safe and sound.'

The older brother became angry and refused to go in. So his father went out and pleaded with him. But he answered his father, 'Look! All these years I've been slaving for you and never disobeyed your orders. Yet you never gave me even a young goat so I could celebrate with my friends. But when this son of yours who has squandered your property with prostitutes comes home, you kill the fattened calf for him!'

'My son,' the father said, 'you are always with me, and everything I have is yours. But we had to celebrate and be glad, because this brother of yours was dead and is alive again; he was lost and is found.'

Luke 15:25-32

Now we focus on a right old misery! I know this isn't the familiar part of the Prodigal Son story but, whereas the lost son who came home to a loving and waiting father has a marvellous lesson for someone who isn't a Christian, the dreary elder brother has something important to say to those of us who are. Although I think of this guy as a Christian, he is one who's totally lost sight of what his father has done for him and given him. Basically he thinks he's had a raw deal. His father hasn't even given him a young goat. What a liberty, when that jerk of a kid brother is having a party! I suppose he'd taken everything for granted. His father's love, his father's provision, and one day his father's inheritance. By any standards, he was a wealthy man but here he is, acting like a bitter, deprived outsider.

Many of us Christians need to wake up to the fact that God, our Father, has given us so much. We have 'immeasurable riches', to use Paul's phrase, not only in this life but in the life to come. And physically too, compared to so much of the world, we're well off, to say the least. Even clean water from our taps sets us in a class apart compared to the world's majority. Christians, I tell you, we are privileged people — and that's a fair-sized understatement. Yet, as I say, so many of us live like spiritual paupers, with little to sustain ourselves, let alone share with others. It's as though the spark of excitement and gratitude has been snuffed out, and complaints and grumbles come to our lips much quicker than praise or joy.

While we're checking our perspectives, remember too that we deserve nothing. The elder son actually thought he'd earned favours. 'All these years I've been slaving for you,' he whined, 'and never disobeyed your orders.' 'I've taught for years in Sunday School,' we might argue today. 'I've served endless cups of tea, always been at meetings early to put out the chairs. Surely I've earned some special consideration. I've done so much more than others.' You younger Christians, still at school, might get all indignant and reckon that going to the Christian Union and being reasonably conscientious about homework are bound to notch up a few good points!

And Jesus said, 'When you've done all that is commanded of you, say "We're not worthy servants. We've only done what was our duty."'

The elder son was a guy who thought he deserved a lot and reckoned he had nothing. In fact he deserved nothing and had everything. Do you see yourself mirrored there just a little? Then look how the father responded to his complaining, ungrateful son. Personally, I'd have told him in no uncertain terms to get lost and only come back when he was in a better frame of mind. But that wasn't the father's way. There was no anger, no reproach, only love and reassurance for someone who, deep down, was still insecure. 'My son, you are with me always.' In that gentle reply there's a reminder of who he was. Permanently, absolutely securely, come what may, the son of his father. He was in the family and that's how it would be for always.

LOOKING FORWARD TO TOMORROW

'For I know the plans I have for you,' declares the LORD, 'plans to prosper you and not to harm you, plans to give you hope and a future. Then you will call upon me and come and pray to me, and I will listen to you. You will seek me and find me when you seek me with all your heart.

I will be found by you,' declares the LORD, 'and will bring you back from captivity. I will gather you from all the nations and places where I have banished you,' declares the LORD, 'and will bring you back to the place from which I carried you into exile.'

Jeremiah 29:11-14

A friend of mine, Garth Hewitt, has taken that phrase — 'a future and a hope' — and used it as the title of a really fantastic song. It's difficult to imagine what life must be like for those whose tomorrow is bleak and hopeless. Nothing to live for, no prospect of improvement or change, just an animal-like fight for survival. I know there are millions in our world like that, living in developing countries, where poverty is crippling and life is cheap. In no way is that God's plan for those He created and loves and, with all the world's potential resources, it needn't be like that.

But there are people much nearer to home who, while better off physically, still only despair over the future. There's no incentive or purpose, no reason or goal. Tomorrow has nothing to offer.

That's tragic but it's also unnecessary. The Bible teaches that God has planned the most fantastic future for us if only we'll allow ourselves to be part of it and, instead of a dead end ahead, we can take on board what is described elsewhere as a 'sure and certain hope'. Of course, if my career collapsed about me all of a sudden, I'd be really disappointed, but it wouldn't be the end of the world and I wouldn't be suicidal. Overriding everything is the conviction that God has a purpose for me which is a million times better than anything I could carve out for myself, and ultimately there's a future which is being with God for ever. I don't know exactly what that will be like, but it helps tremendously to get perspectives right.

YOUR BIGGEST DECISION

Later, knowing that all was now completed, and so that the Scripture would be fulfilled, Jesus said, 'I am thirsty.' A jar of wine vinegar was there, so they soaked a sponge in it, put the sponge on a stalk of the hyssop plant, and lifted it to Jesus' lips. When he had received the drink, Jesus said, 'It is finished.' With that, he bowed his head and gave up his spirit.

John 19:28-30

There's a picture in a museum of Jesus hanging on the cross. Above it the caption reads: 'I've done all this for you; what have you done for me?'

The issue of course is whether you believe it was for you. It's probably the biggest decision you'll face in your life — more important even than who you'll marry. In my mid-twenties, I believed and acted on the basis that Jesus' death was personally relevant and that He accomplished at Calvary all that was necessary for my salvation. I took His final words — 'It is finished' — to mean that there was nothing more I or anyone else had to do to put me right with God. There was no favour I had to earn, no further offering that could be made, no pleading or penance that needed to be expressed. Jesus had done it all. God's plan was complete. All that was left for me to do was acknowledge and accept the truth of it and to live out its implications.

Maybe it's worth letting the 'completeness' of your salvation sink in a bit. All the agonising is over and it's as simple as a gift being offered. I know you don't deserve it, but God's love is greater than your badness, and He wants you to receive it nonetheless. Look at it like this. There's nothing, absolutely nothing, you could ever do, no amount of piety or praying, no depth of kindness or generosity, no sacrifice of time or money, that could possibly qualify you for salvation. It's utterly beyond your reach. The sole qualification for you is what Jesus completed once and for all on the cross. It's His death alone that enables me to tell you with total confidence that God has accepted me.

The only song I sing unaccompanied at some of my concerts is 'When I Survey The Wondrous Cross.' Personally I rate that as one of the most beautiful hymns ever, not only because of its great melody but because the lyrics take us direct to the heart of the challenge. Remember the last verse?

'Were the whole realm of nature mine,
that were an offering far too small;
love so amazing, so divine,
demands my soul, my life, my all!'

IT'S ALL OVER

What shall we say, then? Shall we go on sinning, so that grace may increase? By no means! We died to sin; how can we live in it any longer? Or don't you know that all of us who were baptised into Christ Jesus were baptised into his death? We were therefore buried with him through baptism into death in order that, just as Christ was raised from the dead through the glory of the Father, we too may live a new life.

If we have been united with him in his death, we will certainly also be united with him in his resurrection. For we know that our old self was crucified with him so that the body of sin might be rendered powerless, that we should no longer be slaves to sin — because anyone who has died has been freed from sin.

Romans 6:1-7

Can a Christian go on sinning wilfully, deliberately and repeatedly? Sorry, folks, the answer is no. It's a contradiction. As far as the Christian is concerned, sin is dealt with. It belongs to the past and it's no longer master. When we became Christians, we had a new birth, complete with new life and new nature. Consequently, to go on living as we did before is both unnatural and unnecessary and a denial of God's Spirit within us. Now we serve a different Master and have new resources to serve Him well.

O.K., let's be realistic. There will be times when our old self won't lie down and will assert itself in ways that make us ashamed. That's understood. But it's no longer the norm and no longer inevitable. Before we were Christians, sin came easily and naturally but that's not true any more. Sin is now like some foreign body or irritant maybe, but it has no rightful place and is no more a significant or influential part of our character.

Ask yourself whether you enjoy doing what you know displeases God. If you're a Christian, you'll hate it and know it's incongruous. If it doesn't bother you, then take care — you're playing dangerous games.

TEST YOUR TEMPERATURE

I know your deeds, that you are neither cold not hot. I wish you were either one or the other! So, because you are lukewarm — I am about to spit you out of my mouth. You say, 'I am rich; I have acquired wealth and do not need a thing.' But you do not realise that you are wretched, pitiful, poor, blind and naked. I counsel you to buy from me gold refined in the fire, so that you can become rich; and white clothes to wear, so that you can cover your shameful nakedness; and salve to put on your eyes, so that you can see. Those whom I love I rebuke and discipline. So be earnest and repent.

Revelation 3:15-19

I wonder what your temperature is? Your spiritual temperature, I mean. If you're on the boil for God — all raring to go and wanting to serve Him as best you can — that's great. And what a tonic it is to meet Christians like that in the middle of a long and tiring concert tour!

If you're a cold Christian, who can't seem to summon up much enthusiasm for God these days, then maybe it's time you started to think through your family responsibilities and about that Father of yours who's never stopped loving you for one instant.

But what if you're lukewarm? Apathetic, not bothered. Indifferent — apart, that is, from an occasional visit to church when there's something exciting happening (which isn't often!). As far as God is concerned, that's worse than being frozen. And, whereas He must delight in the 'hot' and weep over the 'cold', He is only angered by those of us who merely give Him a casual nod when it suits us.

It's really quite a sober warning, and the idea of being spat out of God's mouth implies, to me, absolute rejection.

'I don't need God,' people say; 'I'm O.K. without Him and quite self-sufficient, thank you very much.' I wonder how many people think like that. Often they seem, on the face of it, so confident and sometimes more 'successful', by worldly standards, than many Christians. But what a different story from God's perspective! 'Wretched, pitiful, poor, blind and naked' — that's how God describes them, and I guess that's a pretty unenviable position.

As I say, how about checking the spiritual thermometer?

A REASON TO BELIEVE

Who is going to harm you if you are eager to do good? But even if you should suffer for what is right, you are blessed. 'Do not fear what they fear; do not be frightened.' But in your hearts set apart Christ as Lord. Always be prepared to give an answer to everyone who asks you to give the reason for the hope that you have. But do this with gentleness and respect, keeping a clear conscience, so that those who speak maliciously against your good behaviour in Christ may be ashamed of their slander.

1 Peter 3:13-16

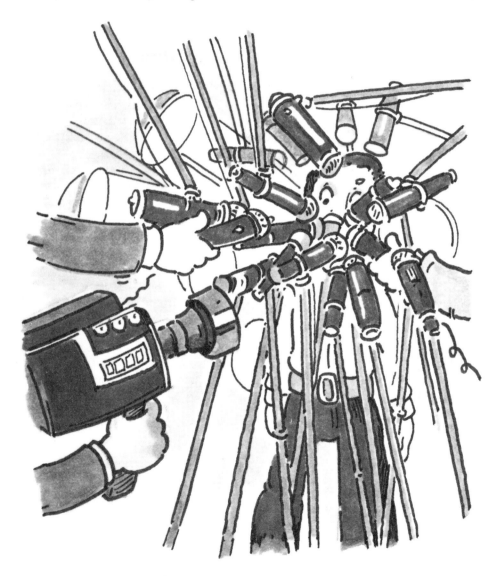

I find it difficult to memorise large chunks of the Bible, but there's a verse here that leaps to my mind almost daily: 'Always be ready to give a reason for what we believe.' (Well, that's the version according to Cliff!)

Over the years that's taken on special significance as I've been pummelled almost mercilessly by press, students and public about what and why I believe. Often the questions have been difficult and to some there are no adequate answers. But being able to support our faith with reason is important and, I promise you, it doesn't demand a degree course in theology to do it.

When people know you're a Christian, they *will* ask questions, whether you like it or not. The only difference between you and me is that your conversations are likely to be less public. People are fascinated by someone else's faith and often they privately envy the peace and purpose they see in a committed Christian.

We owe it to God, to others and to ourselves to have a reasoned Christianity and to have the courage to speak about it when the opportunities come — not in a superior 'know-all' aggressive way, though (never resort to spiritual 'bullying'), but with gentleness and respect. In that way you reinforce what you say.

University degrees aren't needed, not even an A-level, but I do think that Christians should explore and discover as much about their faith as possible. That means reading books occasionally and making a serious attempt to dig into the Bible, rather than just flicking eyes over a few verses while our minds are half asleep. That sort of 'let's get it over with quick' approach will equip you for little, and certainly won't help at times when faith is under pressure.

Naturally I hope that talking about my faith and being 'prepared to give an answer' may prove helpful to others. One thing I do know is that it's proved incredibly helpful to me. Time and time again I've been put on the spot and made to think and, if I've not had an answer there and then, I've gone home, done some reading maybe, or talked with other Christian friends, so that next time I'd be a better ambassador.

One last thing: it says *'always* be prepared'. Sometimes we won't feel like talking. Sometimes we'll be embarrassed, sometimes too nervous maybe, or too tired. Sometimes we'll be in a hurry and think there are more important things to do. In actual fact, I doubt whether many things could be more important than sharing Jesus with someone who doesn't know Him. So be on the alert and, when opportunities come and the green lights flash, offer a little SOS prayer and tell them what you know. You'll be surprised what God can put in your mind and on your lips.

NOT SO STUPID!

Brothers, think of what you were when you were called. Not many of you were wise by human standards; not many were influential; not many were of noble birth. But God chose the foolish things of the world to shame the wise; God chose the weak things of the world to shame the strong. He chose the lowly things of this world and the despised things — and the things that are not — to nullify the things that are, so that no-one may boast before him. It is because of him that you are in Christ Jesus, who has become for us wisdom from God — that is, our righteousness, holiness and redemption. Therefore, as it is written: 'Let him who boasts boast in the Lord.'

1 Corinthians 1:26-31

I'm always amazed how often God uses simple, apparently familiar ideas to get through to intelligent, academic people. Now I'm not in the brainy category, as you'll have realised, but, in spite of that, things which to my mind seem pretty basic and obvious have been regarded as clever and even profound by those who would knock spots off me back in the classroom!

I remember saying something on a recent T.V. show about why it was better not to live together before marriage. As far as I recall, it was all common sense, and what the Bible teaches quite clearly anyway. However, I received a great letter from a lady who was apparently impressed by the reasoning and who, despite a cultured background, had never appreciated what she described as 'the pure wisdom' of it.

So don't be afraid of your simplicity. Of course that mustn't be an excuse for not studying the Bible and trying to get to grips with what it teaches — but don't be daunted by other people's intelligence. You may be in for a shock or two! Some of those seemingly clever theories that I'm constantly hearing at dinner parties, and that I guess you hear at school, in the office, or even over the garden fence, may well fall apart in the light of your 'fool's wisdom'.

FILTHY RAGS

Since ancient times no-one has
* heard,*
* no ear has perceived,*
no eye has seen any God
* besides you,*
* who acts on behalf of those*
* who wait for him.*
You come to the help of those
* who gladly do right,*
* who remember your ways.*
But when we continued to sin
* against them,*
* you were angry.*
How then can we be saved?

All of us have become like one
* who is unclean,*
* and all our righteous acts*
* are like filthy rags;*
we all shrivel up like a leaf,
* and like the wind our sins*
* sweep us away.*
No-one calls on your name
* or strives to lay hold of you;*
for you have hidden your face
* from us*
* and made us waste away*
* because of our sins.*

Isaiah 64:4-7

I wonder if you can spot the flaw in this argument: 'The important thing in life is to be a good neighbour. If you're willing to do a good turn, support a charity, steer clear of trouble, and pay your taxes, you'll be O.K.' I often hear that sort of view, admittedly from very good people most of the time, but what they're saying is that, as long as you're a decent law-abiding citizen, Jesus doesn't matter. The truth is of course that He does matter, even to the most generous and neighbourly of people. The mistake is to think we can earn our way into God's good books — that by being 'decent', by giving to charity, by visiting old people or whatever, we'll qualify for any after-life that there might be. Admittedly, the 'earning your way' principle has its appeal but from man's perspective, not God's. Very conveniently it ignores one crucial ingredient in all our characters, and that is sin. You can be the biggest benefactor, and the most considerate and generous of neighbours, but still carry within you that inherited tendency to do what you shouldn't and ignore what you should. In our honest moments, we have to admit it. We're not perfect, and whatever it is that keeps us from perfection is sin. No matter how 'good' we try to be, we'll never obliterate it. It remains a frustration and, much more seriously, an obstacle which separates us from a God who *is* perfect and holy and just.

As far as God is concerned, says Isaiah, all our 'righteous acts' — all those things which we'd chalk up to our credit — are like 'filthy rags'. They count for nothing. God is unimpressed.

That's why Jesus matters. To the best of neighbours and most decent of citizens, Jesus matters — because only He can deal with the sin, put right our relationship with God, and ensure that those good and thoughtful deeds become not only acceptable to God but actually delight Him.

WHAT MUST I DO?

About midnight Paul and Silas were praying and singing hymns to God, and the other prisoners were listening to them. Suddenly there was such a violent earthquake that the foundations of the prison were shaken. At once all the prison doors flew open, and everybody's chains came loose. The jailer woke up, and when he saw the prison doors open, he drew his sword and was about to kill himself because he thought the prisoners had escaped. But Paul shouted, 'Don't harm yourself! We are all here!'

The jailer called for lights, rushed in and fell trembling before Paul and Silas. He then brought them out and asked, 'Men, what must I do to be saved?'

They replied, 'Believe in the Lord Jesus and you will be saved — you and your household.' Then they spoke the word of the Lord to him and to all the others in his house. At that hour of the night the jailer took them and washed their wounds; then immediately he and all his family were baptised. The jailer brought them into his house and set a meal before them, and the whole family was filled with joy, because they had come to believe in God.

Acts 16:25-34

I can't think why one of those multi-million-dollar film epics hasn't been made about the book of Acts. It's an amazing adventure story — action, suspense, crime, escape — all the ingredients of a box office smash. Maybe there was one, and I was out at the time! These verses from Chapter 16 are just a sampler and, if you're surprised that the Bible can be so easy to read, then try starting at the beginning of Acts and tackling the whole story. You won't get bogged down, and the way the church was started, in the teeth of really vicious opposition, is quite a story. Some have suggested that a better title for the book would have been 'The Acts of the Apostles and of the Holy Spirit', for it's clearly about a partnership. The apostles would have got nowhere on their own, that's for sure, and, if it weren't for the likes of Peter and John, Stephen and Paul and the rest, I'm not sure how God would have launched His church in the first place. But then He always seems to use people to work out His plans for the world.

Anyway, back to the plot. I bet the jailer had no idea that his question would be the subject of thousands of Christian sermons delivered around the world over the centuries! 'What must I do to be saved?' I don't suppose you could ask anything more basic or crucial. But although Paul gave such a clear answer, and although the Bible elaborates on that answer, I'm still surprised how vague and uncertain so many folk remain. 'Is it a matter of going to church?' 'Do I sign something?' 'Is there anything to pay?' 'Do I have to be good?' And so on. Despite all the teaching and despite all that's been written and spoken, the same questions are asked over and over again. And some search in vain for their salvation, in drink or drugs or strange sects and cults, ignoring God's way, which is on free offer and under their very noses.

①

⑪

⑭

If the question is all-important, the answer is even more so. 'Believe in the Lord Jesus,' said Paul, 'and you will be saved.' It couldn't be less complicated, could it? It's *your* trust in Jesus' ability. That's it in a nutshell — too simple or too incredible for some, but not for the jailer and his family. As Paul explained to them about Jesus and what He had done, each one trusted and began a new relationship and a new life.

And, at the risk of sounding like a preacher — which, if you've heard me speak, you'll know I'm not! — there are two little details worth noticing. Firstly, Paul told the jailer with absolute certainty that he would be saved. Not 'you might be' or 'you stand a chance if you toe the line'. It was 'believe and you *will*'. It's on the cards that that jailer may have been the biggest rogue around. He could have had a prison record himself as long as your arm. Paul couldn't possibly have known. The point is that the man's background and past record didn't matter a scrap. What Paul did know was that God loved him, that Jesus died for him, and that the man wanted salvation. He didn't have to qualify, there was no personality test, no I.Q. check. God would accept him there and then, just as he was.

Remember that. God has no rejects, only a one hundred per cent pass list.

Secondly, the whole family put on black suits and looked like death warmed up. Sorry . . . I'll start again! It says they were 'filled with joy because they had come to believe in God'. I'm not surprised. If someone tells you that Christianity is a killjoy faith, tell him from me and the jailer and his family that it just ain't true!

BRAND NEW SONG

Therefore, if anyone is in Christ, he is a new creation; the old has gone, the new has come! All this is from God, who reconciled us to himself through Christ and gave us the ministry of reconciliation: that God was reconciling the world to himself in Christ, not counting men's sins against them. And he has committed to us the message of reconciliation. We are therefore Christ's ambassadors, as though God were making his appeal through us. We implore you on Christ's behalf: Be reconciled to God. God made him who had no sin to be sin for us, so that in him we might become the righteousness of God.

2 Corinthians 5:17-21

There's enough in these four verses to write a book about, let alone a few sentences. Talk about maximum meaning with minimum words! I don't know where to begin, but here are three things about Christians that make an impact on me.

1. Christians are given new lives and are 'new creations'. Cleverly, someone put it like this: 'Christianity is more than a new start in life; it's a new life to start.' There's a big difference. New starts are what we do — or try to do. New Year resolutions and all that, and, as a rule, they're disasters. New lives, on the other hand, are outside our control. They have to be given us by someone else, just like our physical life. A famous Hollywood actress, who committed suicide some years ago, left a sad note to the effect that she had 'a desire to be made all over again'. Presumably no-one had told her that that's just what Jesus can do and that He's in the business of life-changing, as well as life-saving.

2. Christians must be God's ambassadors, and you know what an ambassador is — a representative of the king or queen in a foreign country. It's a huge privilege and a massive responsibility. Our ambassadors virtually take the place of the Queen in her absence in countries around the world. It's as though she is present through them, and that's exactly the role of the Christian ambassador. God's present in this world through us. That is His way of working. We're ambassadors of the King, to proclaim His message with our mouths and to reflect His wishes, His standards and His love through our lives.

3. Christians can share in Jesus' sinlessness and righteousness. I've boggled about that elsewhere, because for me it's still one of the most incredible parts of our faith. I know what I'm like and what I deserve; yet because of what He has done, Jesus' righteousness can and does cover me. That, and only that, makes me acceptable to God. For anyone who thinks he's beyond the pale, the news is that you aren't. If you're still carrying your sin around, then, right, you are unacceptable. God is holy, and holiness and sin can't relate. But you can hump that sin on to Jesus; He's dealt with it to release us. The daft thing about humans is that sometimes they prefer their captivity.

LOVE — THE REAL DEFINITION

If I speak in the tongues of men and of angels, but have not love, I am only a resounding gong or a clanging cymbal. If I have the gift of prophecy and can fathom all mysteries and all knowledge, and if I have a faith that can move mountains, but have not love, I am nothing. If I give all I possess to the poor and surrender my body to the flames, but have not love, I gain nothing.

Love is patient, love is kind. It does not envy, it does not boast, it is not proud. It is not rude, it is not self-seeking, it is not easily angered, it keeps no record of wrongs. Love does not delight in evil but rejoices with the truth. It always protects, always trusts, always hopes, always perseveres.

1 Corinthians 13:1-7

This is where I get a bit red-faced and admit to contributing my two-penn'orth towards the devaluing of the word 'love'. Pop songs dwell on the subject incessantly and, if you deleted every love song from pop history, I guess there'd be no record industry left. Whereas I would hope that my love songs have been honest and perhaps more light-hearted, there's no doubt that a good many so-called 'love lyrics' have distorted and trivialised the most fantastic and beautiful of all God's gifts. Love and lust seem to have become confused, despite the fact that they're virtual opposites. Love is selfless and is interested in the good of the other. Lust is entirely selfish and couldn't care less for anyone else.

The word rolls so easily and glibly off our tongues as well, although maybe that's partly due to our language problems. I 'love' my dogs, I say, and then use exactly the same word to describe my feelings for God and my family. Obviously it means different things in different contexts. But when we apply it to someone and say, 'I love you', it is important that we know what we're meaning.

There's no better definition than here in 1 Corinthians 13. To my mind it's the ultimate, definitive love lyric. Forget the pop songs and the mushy romantic stories in teenage magazines. They pale into spineless insignificance beside this. 'Patient, kind, trusting, protective.' Measure it against your understanding of love and then realise that it isn't a term confined to romantic man/woman relationships but is a quality that the Christian is required to display to all around him. And Paul goes so far as to say that without love like this we're worthless. We may be the most brainy, the most witty, the most talented, even the most religious of people, but without love we count for nothing.

If you're like me, you'll doubt if you're capable of showing that level of love to others, and basically that's right — it is beyond us. But it isn't beyond Jesus. He loves us like that. He loves you and me like that. And the amazing thing is that He can implant that very same quality of love in the life of a Christian. If you think about it, it makes sense. When we become Christians and ask Jesus into our lives, His love comes with Him and potentially He is able to love others through us. Our job is to allow Him to use us and work in us, so that when we meet others they'll get a glimpse of a God who loves them too.

WITH THE EYES OF A CHILD

People were bringing little children to Jesus to have him touch them, but the disciples rebuked them. When Jesus saw this, he was indignant. He said to them, 'Let the little children come to me, and do not hinder them, for the kingdom of God belongs to such as these. I tell you the truth, anyone who will not receive the kingdom of God like a little child will never enter it.' And he took the children in his arms, put his hands on them and blessed them.

Mark 10:13-16

There's all the difference in the world between being childish and being childlike, and obviously Jesus didn't mean that we have to act like a baby when we become Christians. Maybe that's where another of those misunderstandings started. 'It's good for kids, all that Sunday School stuff, but I've grown out of it.' Actually, the reverse is true. We don't grow out of Christianity, we grow into it!

I have nine nieces and nephews altogether and, I promise you, when they're all together it's murder — or very nearly. I'm sat upon, punched, pummelled, bounced and ridden on, and when it's over I look like Worzel Gummidge and feel like his grandad. I love them all dearly and have had tremendous fun playing around on holiday and at home.

Two characteristics come to mind when I think of them and of what Jesus meant when He said that we have to receive the Kingdom of God like a little child. Firstly, they're so very trusting. One of my nieces has a terrifying habit of launching herself at me from the top of the garden steps. It doesn't occur to her for one instant that I might drop her or let her be hurt. Uncle Cliff is there, Uncle Cliff loves me, therefore no need to be afraid. It's simple logic but true nonetheless. And I suspect that Jesus thought, 'If only the grown-ups would trust me in the same way.' His arms are more reliable and more secure than mine. His love is more infinite, more enduring than mine. The trouble is that, as we grow older, our trust is less easily given. Our society and its pressures make us suspicious and cynical. And even if we long to be trusting, something inside asks, 'What's the catch?' Instead of reaching out, we withdraw and pretend it's better to be self-sufficient.

Secondly, my nieces and nephews — and I'm sure they're no different from other children — seem to live in a world of straight-forward blacks and whites. Things are either good or bad, nice or nasty, fun or boring. There aren't many in-betweens, few shades of grey, and that makes decision-making so much easier. The issues are clear and there's no clutter to get in the way. 'Today we're visiting the zoo.' Weather, train strikes, granny's bad leg, admission prices, lunch — all potential complications for Mum and Dad — are irrelevant for the kids. What matters is the zoo — priority number one!

Do you see what Jesus meant? So often we adults have our minds so cluttered up that what really matters in life is blurred and obscured. We can't see the wood for the trees. We can't see Jesus for ifs and buts and maybes. Don't be too proud to be childlike. Encountering Jesus doesn't mean intellectual suicide; just avoid the blind alleys, that's all.

WEIGHT-LIFTING

Therefore, since we are surrounded by such a great cloud of witnesses, let us throw off everything that hinders and the sin that so easily entangles, and let us run with perseverance the race marked out for us. Let us fix our eyes on Jesus, the author and perfector of our faith, who for the joy set before him endured the cross, scorning its shame, and sat down at the right hand of the throne of God. Consider him who endured such opposition from sinful men, so that you will not grow weary and lose heart.

Hebrews 12:1-3

———————

Athletics was a pretty arduous business, by all accounts, in New Testament times. The really good runners used to train with heavy weights tied around their legs and bodies, the idea being that, when they took these off just before a race, their limbs would discover a new freedom and they would be able to sprint like the wind.

Do you understand the illustration? The writer here is comparing the Christian life to a race and, in order to run well, we need to get rid of everything that will hinder and spoil. Sometimes it isn't easy, I know, to get shot of some sin that troubles us over and over again, but there are some 'weights' which we deliberately cling on to, for the simple reason that we prefer to keep them.

There's a story that I've always thought a bit dubious about monkey-trapping in India. Apparently they used to catch them by shoving a whole banana into a milk bottle and dangling it in a tree. The monkey would come along, see the banana, stick its little paw through the neck of the bottle, and grab the fruit. Obviously, with a fistful of banana, it couldn't pull its paw out again, so there it stayed, preferring to be trapped rather than to let go. Well, that's what I was told, anyway.

But I guess there must be many of us whose witness for Jesus is spoiled because of some sin in our lives that we're unwilling to let go. We know it's holding us back but, instead of releasing our grip, we stubbornly cling on. Maybe it's time now to let go and be free, like letting go of the weights.

There's another thing about a race. From the instant it begins, the experienced athlete will fix his sights on one point and one point only. That's the finishing tape. If he's distracted and turns his head to look at an opponent, he can lose a vital fraction of a second and lose the race. Remember how, in 'Chariots of Fire', the Olympic athlete, Harold Abrahams, had exactly that problem to overcome?

Again, what a great parallel. In our Christian race our eyes must be fixed only and always on Jesus. Often the temptation is to look at others, to see how they're doing. A bit better maybe, or not as good. When we do that, we swerve, lose our direction, and the race is lost. For many years I was involved with the Crusaders Union, a network of Bible classes for boys and girls around the country. One of the verses here is the Crusader motto and I can't think of a better one: 'Let's fix our eyes on Jesus'.

A HIGH COST

Dear friends, do not be surprised at the painful trial you are suffering as though something strange were happening to you.
But rejoice that you participate in the sufferings of Christ, so that you may be overjoyed when his glory is revealed. If you are insulted because of the name of Christ, you are blessed, for the Spirit of glory and of God rests on you. If you suffer, it should not be as a murderer or thief or any other kind of criminal, or even as a meddler. However, if you suffer as a Christian, do not be ashamed, but praise God that you bear that name.

1 Peter 4:12-16

Not many of us know what it's like to suffer for being a Christian in Britain. Apart from a bit of leg-pulling and embarrassment at school maybe, and the knowledge that some who know no better regard us as oddballs, there's no real suffering as such to endure. Occasionally we read of a Christian who stands out on some matter of principle and is sent to Coventry by his trade union maybe or, worse still, loses his job. That's grim and, by comparison, being sniggered at is trivial and harmless. But of course it's all a matter of degree. I understand that being mocked is no fun, and schoolmates can be really cruel if we make a stand for Jesus.

But think of those first-century Christians who were prepared to face hungry lions for their faith in a Roman arena. The sort of physical pain they must have gone through doesn't bear thinking about. And, all through history, there have been followers of Jesus who have been persecuted, humiliated, tortured and killed for what they believed. And still today, in certain countries, there is no religious tolerance or freedom, and Christians are banned from holding meetings to pray or to worship. But, despite the risk of fines, imprisonment, and the ruin of career prospects, they ignore the restriction and meet illegally in forests and secret hideaways. I guess few of us know even a fraction of the penalties and the hardship that many contemporary Christians are enduring because of their loyalty and obedience to Jesus. All we can know is that persecution and opposition produce spiritual muscle and, far from Christian life being snuffed out in these places, the church, though relatively small, is strong and energetic and could certainly teach us flabby followers a lesson or two. Also, where there is suffering, there is God's blessing because, in some strange mystical way, suffering for Christ's sake is identified in God's mind with the suffering of Jesus.

I often wonder how I'd shape up under fierce opposition. I'd never know until it happened. Meanwhile, I can only pray for my Christian brothers and sisters who do suffer. That has to be part of the responsibility of the rest of us.

A LITTLE IN LOVE

Hearing that Jesus had silenced the Sadducees, the Pharisees got together. One of them, an expert in the law, tested him with this question: 'Teacher, which is the greatest commandment in the Law?'

Jesus replied: 'Love the Lord your God with all your heart and with all your soul and with all your mind. This is the first and greatest commandment. And the second is like it: "Love your neighbour as yourself." All the Law and the Prophets hang on these two commandments.'

Matthew 22:34-40

'Lord, I love you' is one of the relatively few Christian songs I have written and, after I sang it to an audience in Birmingham on one occasion, I remember someone asking what I meant by 'loving God'. How do we love God? Love has so many facets and shades of meaning — I 'love' the skin off the custard, for instance!

Basically, our love for God comes from recognising how much He loves us and how much He has done for us. When that begins to dawn, we will inevitably feel grateful and will want to obey and worship Him. Now that isn't necessarily plain sailing but at least we have the motivation, and that's the all-important factor.

When it comes to loving our neighbour, by the way, I have a word to say about that somewhere else, but note the bit about loving 'as much as we love ourselves'. Some of us have such a low opinion of ourselves that any love for others doesn't stand a chance. And before you think the Bible is saying it's O.K. to be conceited or big-headed, remember that the only reason we can regard ourselves highly is because God regards us highly. It's remarkable but true nevertheless. Despite what we are, He loves us.

LIVING IN HARMONY

King Solomon, however, loved many foreign women besides Pharoah's daughter — Moabites, Ammonites, Edomites, Sidonians and Hittites. They were from nations about which the LORD had told the Israelites, 'You must not intermarry with them, because they will surely turn your hearts after their gods.' Nevertheless, Solomon held fast to them in love.

The LORD became angry with Solomon because his heart had turned away from the LORD, the God of Israel, who had appeared to him twice. Although he had forbidden Solomon to follow other gods, Solomon did not keep the LORD'S command. So the LORD said to Solomon, 'Since this is your attitude and you have not kept my covenant and my decrees, which I commanded you, I will most certainly tear the kingdom away from you and give it to one of your subordinates.'

1 Kings 11:1-2, 9-11

Here's a tricky one. Undoubtedly wealthy, King Solomon came a cropper, partly because he ignored God's instruction and had relationships with women who didn't share his faith. I know this is way back in Old Testament history, when customs and lifestyles were so different, but nevertheless I believe this underlines an important principle that's still relevant. Elsewhere I've stressed the importance of Christians mixing socially with non-Christians and avoiding exclusive 'holy huddles'. But, in the area of boy/girl, man/woman relationships, it's different. There isn't a scrap of doubt that it's unwise and unhelpful for a Christian boy or a Christian girl to develop a serious relationship with a partner who is not a Christian. It's asking for trouble.

Christian 'agony columns', if there were such things, would be full of tell-tale, real-life testimony to the fact that it doesn't work and that, in nine cases out of ten, if the relationship doesn't break up, the Christian's life slowly evaporates, despite every good intention to the contrary. It's happened again and again, despite the Christian's sincere determination to win the other person for Christ.

I won't dwell on it, and I'm not too good at doing an 'Uncle Cliff', but here's a reminder to young Christians that the Bible warns against being 'unequally yoked' and real-life experience serves only as reinforcement. If it isn't too late, don't let your heart take a trip in that direction.

ME AND MY SHADOW

The apostles performed many miraculous signs and wonders among the people. And all the believers used to meet together in Solomon's Colonnade. No-one else dared join them, even though they were highly regarded by the people. Nevertheless, more and more men and women believed in the LORD and were added to their number. As a result, people brought the sick into the streets and laid them on beds and mats so that at least Peter's shadow might fall on some of them as he passed by. Crowds gathered also from the towns around Jerusalem bringing their sick and those tormented by evil spirits, and all of them were healed.

Acts 5:12-16

I've got to have something in my book about Shadows. Even though we don't work together these days, they'd feel bad if I left them out! The nearest I can get to a mention is this strange little reference to Peter's shadow. Whether people were genuinely healed by it or whether it was a developing superstition, I'm not sure, but there's no doubt it had an influence and it makes me think of the shadows we cast and the influence we have on others.

All of us have some influence, just as all of us cast a shadow. Sometimes — in Peter's case, for instance — it works for good, sometimes its effect is bad. In hot sunny countries, shadows are much in demand. In some open-air stadiums, the most expensive tickets aren't necessarily in the front row, they're in the shade. Then, on the other hand, we know how spooky and frightening shadows can be in horror movies and thrillers. A while back, the driver of a car said the reason for his sudden crash was the shadow of an aeroplane that flashed across the road in front of him. Hardly a helpful shadow.

What's important is that not only do we all have shadows but they're also a projection of what we are. If you're wearing an outrageous hat, there it'll be on your shadow. If you have an equally outrageous pot belly, there's no escape — that'll be there too. I know sometimes we can throw misleading shadows, like those shapes we make with our hands on a wall. Maybe we can make it look like a rabbit or a fox, but a little investigation and the illusion's over.

It's the same in reality. Your influence depends on what you are. An empty dissatisfied life that observes few standards or principles can hardly have a positive or healthy effect on another. Someone who is directionless, heading nowhere in particular, has nothing to offer by way of helpful guidance. A godly life, on the other hand, can only have a godly influence. Personally, the people I'm most happy to have met in my life are the ones who've influenced me for Jesus. There are others I wish I'd avoided — but I'll leave it at that!

PASS THE KIDNEYS!

The body is a unit, though it is made up of many parts; and though all its parts are many, they form one body. So it is with Christ. For we were all baptised by one Spirit into one body — whether Jews or Greeks, slave or free — and we were all given the one Spirit to drink.

Now the body is not made up of one part but of many. If the foot should say, 'Because I am not a hand I do not belong to the body,' it would not for that reason cease to be part of the body. And if the ear should say, 'Because I am not an eye, I do not belong to the body,' it would not for that reason cease to be part of the body. If the whole body were an eye, where would the sense of hearing be? If the whole body were an ear, where would the sense of smell be? But in fact God has arranged the parts in the body, every one of them, just as he wanted them to be. If they were all one part, where would the body be? As it is, there are many parts, but one body.

If one part suffers, every part suffers with it; if one part is honoured, every part rejoices with it.

Now you are the body of Christ, and each one of you is a part of it.

1 Corinthians 12:12-20, 26-27

I suffer every so often with a dodgy disc — of the spinal rather than the vinyl variety. I remember going through a tv series several years ago now with my back strapped in a kind of corset affair. Very un-hip! The doctors tell me that the culprit is one tiny, slightly misshapen vertebra. Tiny maybe, but when it pops out of place my whole body comes out in sympathy and I have to take to the bedroom floor for three or four days. There's no way I can move around.

What a clever illustration this is of Paul's to teach us about the Christian family, or the Body of Christ, or the Church (they all mean the same). Firstly, I see that every individual Christian has some role to play in the life of the church. On the face of it, it may seem a trivial unimportant role but it isn't like that. Every one of us is different, for sure, and we have different gifts and personalities, but every one of us is needed to complete the body. What a silly situation, says Paul, if the eye argued that it was more important than the ear. The fact is that they're both different but both vital.

Sometimes I hear people say, 'I could never do what you do,' and they get discouraged. The point is that they're not supposed to do what I do. They're a different part of the body. Maybe not one of the more visible parts but one that's equally important, tucked away out of view, like my disc! So don't measure yourself against a Billy Graham or a Mother Teresa. You are you, and you have your own unique job to do.

And that's the second principle: when one part fails in its function then the whole body suffers. You know the effect of a bad tooth, for instance. It's only a small part but, if it starts aching, you feel lousy all over. Just remember that, when the church seems to be limping along and looks a bit tired and listless, the reason is sure to be that some of its members aren't healthy or are just not functioning.

So, you hand or toe or muscle or whatever you are, get stuck in there and do your job!

EVERYTHING I NEED

The LORD is my shepherd, I
  shall lack nothing.
He makes me lie down in
  green pastures,
He leads me beside quiet
  waters,
  He restores my soul.
He guides me in paths of
  righteousness
for His name's sake.
Even though I walk
  through the valley of the
  shadow of death,
I will fear no evil,
  for you are with me;
your rod and your staff,
  they comfort me.

You prepare a table before me
  in the presence of my
  enemies.
You anoint my head with oil;
  my cup overflows.
Surely goodness and love will
  follow me
  all the days of my life,
and I will dwell in the house
  of the LORD for ever.

Psalm 23

It all depends on your frame of mind. If you're confident, on top of the world, with no worries or difficulties, then great. But David's Psalm won't be too relevant. Maybe you should come back to it some other time. If life seems a bit bleak, on the other hand, and you're more conscious than usual of your weakness, then this holds so much comfort and reassurance. Just let your mind work around the first phrase — the idea of the Lord being a shepherd, your shepherd. Think of what a shepherd does and how he leads and protects and cares for his flock. I remember driving to my cottage in Wales one year when I nearly ran over a sheep that had somehow squeezed through a wire fence. I stopped, and had just picked it up, to put it back over the wire, when the shepherd appeared and I had the embarrassing job of convincing him that I wasn't stealing it. There must have been hundreds of sheep grazing in the field and on the hillside, but the shepherd was aware of the one that went missing, and it was his responsibility to find it and return it to safety.

The Bible refers to God by several different names, all of which teach separate facets of His character — He is Creator, Provider, Sustainer, Judge, the Holy One, Saviour, and so on. But, of all His names, I think God the Shepherd is the most graphic and lovely. Sheep are silly, wilful creatures, but the shepherd understands them and loves them despite it. Left to themselves,

sheep will wander and stray to where it isn't safe, but the shepherd is watchful and will personally search for even one that goes missing. Sheep haven't the sense even to know what's good for them, and will choke trying to drink fast-running water. The shepherd knows what is best and will lead his sheep to where the water is still and safe and refreshing. Looked after by the shepherd, the sheep is safe and secure.

The comparisons go on, and it's Jesus who points out the ultimate — 'I am the Good Shepherd,' He says in John's Gospel; 'the Good Shepherd lays down His life for the sheep.'

There was once a competition for the best public reading of Psalm 23. Among the competitors were an actor and an elderly clergyman. The actor recited the Psalm powerfully and without a flaw. Eventually it was the minister's turn and, in a rather faltering voice, he began, 'The Lord is my shepherd...' and so on.

Eventually the judges put their heads together and announced that their prize went to the clergyman. 'I'm sorry you didn't win,' said the old man to the actor; 'I think you deserved to.' 'Not at all,' the actor replied quietly. 'There was one big difference: I know the Psalm, but you know the Shepherd.'

WHO IS THIS MAN?

Then he got into the boat and his disciples followed him. Without warning, a furious storm came up on the lake, so that the waves swept over the boat. But Jesus was sleeping. The disciples went and woke him, saying, 'Lord, save us! We're going to drown!'

He replied, 'You of little faith, why are you so afraid?' Then he got up and rebuked the winds and the waves, and it was completely calm.

The men were amazed and asked, 'What kind of man is this? Even the winds and the waves obey him!'

Matthew 8:23-27

This miracle of Jesus speaks for itself and there's little I can add, other than that it underlines for me His claim to be God's Son. Other men have been healers; no-one else has had authority over the winds and the seas. But do I believe it happened, that's the question. Not just this miracle, but the others in the Bible. Living in a scientific age, can a reasonably intelligent person accept the miraculous? Goodness knows how many times I've been asked that, and it's come from kids at school, students at university, and businessmen at dinners and conferences. It's a real old chestnut and I always answer it in the only way I know how.

Yes, I do believe in Jesus' miracles — all of them — for what, to me, seems a very logical reason. Through His words, Jesus claimed to be no less than the divine Son of God. Elsewhere the Bible teaches that Jesus has equality with God the Father, that through Him all things were created, and that there was never a time when He didn't exist. In the book of Revelation, Jesus claims: 'I am the Alpha and the Omega, the First and the Last, the Beginning and the End.' Now, I don't understand the mystery of the Trinity — the exact relationship between God the Father, God the Son, and God the Holy Spirit is beyond me, and that business of 'One in Three and Three in One' I find totally confusing. Having said that, I can feebly grasp the certainty that Jesus on earth had the nature and all the potential power and authority of God. In no way was He just another man, no matter how gifted or exceptional.

Sorry to get 'heavy', but do you see why it's important in understanding and accepting His miracles? If we were talking about Joe Bloggs, the fishmonger, who stilled the storm, or even some great world leader, come to that, it would be ridiculous and anyone who believed it would need his head examined. But it isn't Joe Bloggs or any world leader. It's God's Son, whose nature is unique; and I don't know about you, but I'd be more surprised, and even a little disappointed, if God's Son didn't achieve the miraculous. I expect Jesus to have an authority over and beyond yours or mine. I expect His life to complement what He said and to square with what the rest of the Bible teaches. I expect to see Jesus demonstrate at least a little of that whole new spiritual realm that our minds understand so imperfectly.

So then if you ask me, 'How did Jesus still the storm?' sorry, I haven't a clue. If you ask me, 'Do you believe that the *Lord* Jesus did it?' then yes, I haven't a shred of doubt.

LIVING PROOF

On the first day of the week, very early in the morning, the women took the spices they had prepared and went to the tomb. They found the stone rolled away from the tomb, but when they entered, they did not find the body of the Lord Jesus. While they were wondering about this, suddenly two men in clothes that gleamed like lightning stood beside them. In their fright the women bowed down with their faces to the ground, but the men said to them, 'Why do you look for the living among the dead? He is not here; he has risen! Remember how he told you, while he was still with you in Galilee: "The Son of Man must be delivered into the hands of sinful men, be crucified and on the third day be raised again." ' Then they remembered his words.

Luke 24:1-8

Kept under lock and key in some Eastern holy place is a tooth reputed to have belonged to Buddha, founder of the Buddhist faith. Many flock to see it as a visible reminder of their great leader and teacher.

Hunt and dig and sift as they might, no-one ever found any mortal remains of Jesus. The nearest experts have come is to claim that a shroud — a length of cloth which was wrapped around a body — may well have been the one used for Jesus. You'll have read about the Shroud of Turin. Some think it could well be the actual cloth; others doubt it. Some say it doesn't matter.

The point is that on Easter Sunday Jesus rose from the dead — God's seal of approval that Jesus' work was accomplished and totally accepted. There are no remains of Jesus, for the evidence of His rising is overwhelming and compelling, not only from Biblical accounts but from Roman documents of the period. A useful book spelling out that evidence is *Man Alive* by Michael Green.

Clearly the sight of those empty grave-clothes and the rolled-back stone lifted the disciples from despair to cloud nine. Maybe some of the things Jesus said to them, which they didn't really grasp at the time, came rushing back. So this wasn't the end of the story — some dreadful anti-climax fizzle. It was the beginning — of what they weren't sure, but Jesus was back and that was all that mattered. Without Him they were futureless nobodies; with Him they could turn the world upside-down.

It wasn't long before the early church realised that Resurrection Sunday was the cornerstone of their faith, and it was natural to transfer the weekly Sabbath — God's holy day — from Saturday to Sunday, so that each week, not just each year at Easter, became a celebration of Jesus being alive and of death being conquered.

Don't tell me — I know that many church services are more like weekly funerals than celebrations. But they're not all like that, I promise. Just find a fellowship where the people recognise and demonstrate that Jesus is alive and well.

'May you live to dance on your own grave,' sings Garth Hewitt. Work that out for yourself!

RED HERRINGS!

As I urged you when I went into Macedonia, stay there in Ephesus so that you may command certain men not to teach false doctrines any longer nor to devote themselves to myths and endless genealogies. These promote controversies rather than God's work — which is by faith. The goal of this command is love, which comes from a pure heart and a good conscience and a sincere faith. Some have wandered away from these and turned to meaningless talk. They want to be teachers of the law, but they do not know what they are talking about or what they so confidently affirm.

1 Timothy 1:3-7

Not all religious discussion is useful. I've discovered that to my cost, after being cornered for hours listening to people's way-out theories on how life began and what God is like. It's incredible what they come up with. 'Star Trek' isn't in it for pure fantasy and imagination! One of the 'in' topics for speculation today, for instance, is reincarnation — that we all have to go through a series of different lives, and the way we live in this one determines how we'll return in the next. It's fascinating and you could talk for hours about it and get precisely nowhere, because one view is only as good and valid as the next. It's ingenious as a theory but that's all it is — a theory. Jesus certainly didn't teach reincarnation and the Bible makes no reference to it. It's what some people think might happen and, when you get into those realms where man is his own authority, well, the sky's the limit!

In no way am I suggesting that Christians should be disrespectful of other people's sincerely held views, and Paul isn't suggesting that to Timothy either. But often, in this kind of discussion, the most vigorous talkers have no genuine views of their own at all and talk very largely for the sake of being controversial. Often they're not interested in listening to a Christian viewpoint, neither are they prepared to reason Biblically or historically.

The Bible's advice is 'don't bother'. Don't waste your breath. For every one who wants only to spout his own ideas, there are another dozen who are genuinely interested to discern the truth. O.K., let's have a chuckle with the speculators by all means, but let's save our main conversation time for those who, although perhaps holding different views from our own, are serious in their thinking and honest in their motives.

SALT AND LIGHT

'You are the salt of the earth. But if the salt loses its saltiness, how can it be made salty again? It is no longer good for anything, except to be thrown out and trampled by men.

'You are the light of the world. A city on a hill cannot be hidden. Neither do people light a lamp and put it under a bowl. Instead they put it on its stand, and it gives light to everyone in the house. In the same way, let your light shine before men, that they may see your good deeds and praise your Father in heaven.

Matthew 5:13-16

Whenever I think of someone being 'salt', I think of a schoolboy who was sadly killed in an accident. I didn't know him personally, but heard that after his death his teachers and schoolfriends put up a little memorial with the words: 'When he was with us, it was easier to be good'. What a great way to be remembered — and what a fantastic explanation of what Jesus meant.

Salt has the effect of preventing things from going bad, and improving the flavour, and this boy's life had just that sort of influence on those he met. They lived just that little bit better because of him — not because they were instructed or forced, but because they wanted to. There are many who, because of their ugly language maybe or because of their anti-social attitudes, tend to drag others down. Theirs is a destructive influence. The Christian's role is to make life better, healthier certainly, and a pinch more tasty!

As for being a light, that's simple. Light gets rid of darkness and enables us to see, so again it boils down to a matter of influence. I've often been asked what I'd like for an epitaph. I'd be more than happy with the one given to that schoolboy, but just as good would be that, because of me, others had a better view of Jesus. I really couldn't ask for more than that.

Too bad that so often our salt is insipid and our light is dim. Instead of being out and about in the classroom, in studios and on factory floors, in shops and offices and colleges, influencing and affecting the world for Christ, we chicken out and choose to limit our Christian profile to church, where it's easy — and where it's expected of us anyway!

TWO KINDS OF FRUIT

So I say, live by the Spirit, and you will not gratify the desires of the sinful nature. For the sinful nature desires what is contrary to the Spirit, and the Spirit what is contrary to the sinful nature. They are in conflict with each other, so that you do not do what you want. But if you are led by the Spirit, you are not under law.

The acts of the sinful nature are obvious: sexual immorality, impurity and debauchery; idolatry and witchcraft; hatred, discord, jealousy, fits of rage, selfish ambition, dissensions, factions and envy; drunkenness, orgies, and the like. I warn you, as I did before, that those who live like this will not inherit the kingdom of God.

But the fruit of the Spirit is love, joy, peace, patience, kindness, goodness, faithfulness, gentleness and self-control. Against such things there is no law.

Galatians 5:16-23

Back to internal warfare and those two natures that the Christian has — the old sinful one and the new Jesus force. I guess most of us are more familiar with the first of Paul's lists than the second and, catalogued like this, it makes pretty nasty reading. But pick up any national newspaper and you'll find it all illustrated. The 'acts of the sinful nature' make good news copy!

I often wonder what evidence there is to support the theory of 'gradual improvement' — that, slowly but surely, people are getting better and their moral judgment and social behaviour are on the up and up. Some believe it, despite everything that I see and read to the contrary. I'm no pessimist as far as ultimate world destiny is concerned, for I'm convinced that God remains in control of His world. But I read nothing in the Bible about any automatic improvement in people's make-up, and those who point to a moral decline over the past hundred years — at least in our society — seem to me to be nearer the truth.

Personally, I believe the potential for all the evil things which Paul itemises is present in every one of us, and it's wrong and dangerous to think we're immune. Given different circumstances and situations, Satan can throw the whole gamut of temptation at us, and the fact that maybe to date we've avoided some of the more sensational pitfalls is no reason for pride, and even less for complacency.

But what of the other sort of fruit? One thing's for sure — just as you won't get apples from a chestnut tree, neither can you expect spiritual fruit from a non-spiritual person. There's no way that you and I can artificially create patience, kindness, goodness and so on in our lives by trying. It doesn't happen like that. Those qualities have to emerge naturally and unconsciously from the sort of people we are and, just as our old nature produces selfishness, jealousy, anger and all the rest, without our having to try too hard, so the Holy Spirit in our lives can produce His fruit if we co-operate with Him. I can't love in the way God wants me to love, I can't be gentle and self-controlled and at peace by summoning up reserves of will-power, but if I'm in step with God, then He'll be creating that fruit in me by His Spirit. It will be His doing, not mine.

I've got a pear tree in my garden at home; it gives us a great crop of leaves each year, but not so much as a peep from even one rotten pear. All the potential is there, but presumably there's something wrong with the roots or the soil and the tree isn't being fed or nourished. If you're a bit short on spiritual fruit, apply the parallel. The lesson is obvious.

CHRISTIAN IDENTIKIT

Therefore I urge you, brothers, in view of God's mercy, to offer your bodies as living sacrifices, holy and pleasing to God — which is your spiritual worship.

Love must be sincere. Hate what is evil; cling to what is good. Be devoted to one another in brotherly love. Honour one another above yourselves. Never be lacking in zeal, but keep your spiritual fervour, serving the Lord. Be joyful in hope, patient in affliction, faithful in prayer. Share with God's people who are in need. Practise hospitality.

Bless those who persecute you; bless and do not curse. Rejoice with those who rejoice; mourn with those who mourn. Live in harmony with one another. Do not be proud, but be willing to associate with people of low position. Do not be conceited.

Romans 12:1, 9-16

How about this for a Christian's identikit? Does it resemble you just a bit? It's a far cry from the sandwich-board man proclaiming 'Prepare to meet thy doom', that's for sure. To me, this composite Christian conveys an impression of strength and composure. There's nothing insipid or flabby about the person who's 'zealous, hospitable, patient, sincere' and so on, and it's interesting how the majority of these individual little identification marks relate to attitudes to other people. Certainly we must be faithful in prayer, and joyful and patient, but that's all part and parcel of living in harmony and sharing with neighbours and friends and relatives. So much of Christianity is about living in community and you can't tell me that your neighbourhood wouldn't be a better, happier place if it were full of Christians based on this model. Just think about it. I'm idealistic, I know, but suppose that Paul's 'identikit' described everyone in your town or village. No aggro, no loneliness, no fear, no needless suffering... but then I'm dreaming and I guess we'll have to wait for heaven until we reach perfection like that.

The picture of course is of the Christian who has put himself entirely under God's control, and you might have to revise your ideas about the meaning of worship in the light of this first sentence. Obviously it isn't something you only do in church at certain times on Sundays. It's much much broader and can involve literally everything you do, whether it's a plainly 'religious' activity or not. Worshipping God means that we tell Him and show Him that He is worthy of our best — of our best love, our best work, our best play, our best everything. So painting a picture can become an act of worship (or 'worth-ship') if we do it well 'as unto the Lord'. Singing a song, even a pop song, can become worship if, in my mind, I'm saying, 'Lord, I want this to be for you. It's the very best I can sing because you're worth the best I can give.' Apply that motivation to every action and every responsibility, and the whole of life becomes worship, which gives God pleasure.

PRAYER CHANGES THINGS

But when you pray, do not be like the hypocrites, for they love to pray standing in the synagogues and on the street corners to be seen by men. I tell you the truth, they have received their reward in full. When you pray, go into your room, close the door and pray to your Father, who is unseen. Then your Father, who sees what is done in secret, will reward you. And when you pray, do not keep on babbling like pagans, for they think they will be heard because of their many words. Do not be like them, for your Father knows what you need before you ask him.
This is how you should pray:
'Our Father in heaven,
hallowed be your name,
your kingdom come, your will be done,
on earth as it is in heaven.
Give us today our daily bread.
Forgive us our debts,
as we also have forgiven our debtors.
And lead us not into temptation,
but deliver us from the evil one.'

Matthew 6:5-13

As a rule, I co-operate as best I can with the press, but I always give a point-blank refusal to photographers who want a shot of a group of us praying — maybe before a concert or church meeting. For a start, their motives are likely to be dubious in terms of any eventual 'story', and, secondly, that kind of public piety seems a twentieth-century parallel to what Jesus was warning against. Prayer is the most personal and intimate means of communicating with God and it's hard to imagine how those hypocrites of Jesus' day could use such a fantastic gift for self-display.

People often claim that faith is something personal and private, to be kept to oneself. I don't agree. If no-one spoke about it or shared it, who would ever hear? Not me, for starters! Now, prayer is different. Jesus teaches that it's something we are to do quietly and personally and, although that doesn't rule out Christians praying together (the Bible teaches the importance of that as well), it's vital for every Christian to have his or her very own special prayer link with God. For some, that will mean using a book of prayers — beautiful words, written and prayed by great men and women of God in days past. For others, me included, it will mean just talking to God in our own fumbling way, but sharing our needs and our love very spontaneously. For all of us, it will mean praying from time to time that prayer which Jesus taught and which Christians all over the world regard as the special family prayer. Try and understand the words as you pray, because it's easy to be superstitious and treat it as some kind of magic formula. It isn't, and it's important that we pray with our understanding. Many books have been written about the Lord's Prayer and, if you can get hold of even a simple commentary, you'd be amazed how so much is packed into so relatively few words.

There's a line of a chorus that simply says, 'Prayer changes things'. I'll vouch for that, and the more you pray and chat to Him the more you'll realise that God is a great listener.

NOT ME — JESUS!

They came to John and said to him, 'Rabbi, that man who was with you on the other side of the Jordan — the one you testified about — well, he is baptising, and everyone is going to him.'

To this John replied, 'A man can receive only what is given him from heaven. You yourselves can testify that I said, "I am not the Christ but am sent ahead of him." The bride belongs to the bridegroom. The friend who attends the bridegroom waits and listens for him, and is full of joy when he hears the bridegroom's voice. That joy is mine, and it is now complete. He must become greater; I must become less.'

John 3:26-30

I can just imagine John the Baptist getting frustrated with the crowds who were following him, and saying, 'No, you've got it wrong. It's not me you should be spending time with — it's Him, Jesus. I'm like you, just an ordinary person. Jesus is from God. He's the Messiah. Follow Him.'

It's the easiest thing in my business to get swollen-headed and full of self-importance. There isn't a shred of justification for it because entertainers must be way down the list when it comes to the genuinely important people in society. But it's easy for Christians in any walk of life to seek the limelight. It bolsters our ego to be the focus of attention and it's nice to be a big fish in a small pool. John the Baptist wasn't after the limelight. He wanted that to be centred on Jesus and Jesus alone: 'He must become greater,' he said, 'and I must become less.'

There's a story I heard about the great artist, Leonardo da Vinci. After he had finished his painting of the Last Supper, he showed it to a friend and asked him what he thought. 'It's magnificent,' said the friend. 'Every detail is so perfect, and see how the eye catches that beautiful gold chalice.' With that, da Vinci took up his brush and, with one stroke, totally obliterated the carefully-painted cup. 'I want your eye to go only to Jesus', said da Vinci. 'Anything that distracts from Him must go.'

Before our gospel concerts, a group of us usually get together to pray for a while. One prayer always is that the audience will somehow be able to see beyond me on stage and focus their thinking on the One I try to represent. Anything that distracts from Jesus must go. That applies to my life offstage as well. It must point people to Him, and Cliff Richard mustn't get in the way.

Will you check that out in your life too, if you're a Christian? It's a matter of 'more of Jesus and less of me'. Or might it be vice versa?

YOU KNOW ME BETTER THAN I KNOW MYSELF

O LORD, you have searched
me
and you know me.
You know when I sit and
when I rise;
you perceive my thoughts
from afar.
You discern my going out and
my lying down;
you are familiar with all my
ways.
Before a word is on my tongue
you know it completely, O
LORD.
You hem me in, behind and
before;
you have laid your hand
upon me.
Such knowledge is too
wonderful for me,
too lofty for me to attain.

Where can I go from your
Spirit?
Where can I flee from your
presence?
If I go up to the heavens, you
are there;
if I make my bed in the
depths, you are there.
If I rise on the wings of the
dawn,
if I settle on the far side of
the sea,
even there your hand will
guide me,
your right hand will hold
me fast.

Psalm 139:1-10

In some parts of the world, there are still primitive people who are frightened of their gods. They see them as cruel, cunning powers who are out to punish and destroy, and who can only be appeased by rituals and sacrifices. If only they knew! But even in our society there's a similar superstition. God is like 'Big Brother' — watching to catch us out and make our lives narrow and miserable. It's a strange notion and bears no resemblance at all to the Bible's picture.

For sure, God does watch us. He knows us through and through — every thought we think and every word we say. That song of mine puts it perfectly: 'You know me better than I know myself'. But, far from being a tyrant or big brother in the sky, God watches us as a doting father would watch his newborn babies — with deep love and compassion.

Certainly the idea of an all-knowing and ever-present God didn't scare David. 'Such knowledge is too wonderful for me,' he wrote. I hope it doesn't scare you either, although I can imagine that, if your heart and your relationship with Him aren't right, then it can't be much of a comfort to know you can never escape Him. On the other hand, if you know Him as a loving father, what a fabulous reassurance to have Him always with you. You can jetset to Los Angeles, Australia, Japan or Africa, and His love is still there, unchanging and totally dependable.

I tell you one thing. A mature adult I may be (well, I'm over 21) but to know that 'God's right hand holds me fast' provides a depth of security that I need — and I'm not a bit ashamed to admit it.

CAN'T ASK FOR ANYTHING MORE THAN YOU

To keep me from becoming conceited because of these surpassingly great revelations, there was given me a thorn in my flesh, a messenger of Satan, to torment me. Three times I pleaded with the LORD to take it away from me. But he said to me, 'My grace is sufficient for you, for my power is made perfect in weakness.' Therefore I will boast all the more gladly about my weaknesses, so that Christ's power may rest on me. That is why, for Christ's sake, I delight in weaknesses, in insults, in hardships, in persecutions, in difficulties. For when I am weak, then I am strong.

2 Corinthians 12:7-10

I don't know what Paul's problem was and it doesn't really matter. The point is there were times when he was at the end of his tether and thought he couldn't cope. In these circumstances, the Lord gave him a fantastic, timeless promise that I find myself drawing on again and again until it's become a kind of lifeline. 'My grace (or my enabling power) is sufficient for you.' Not an elaborate promise, but all that Paul and millions of Christians after him have needed to survive some crisis or danger or bad patch in their lives.

A medical friend told me recently that one of the most widely prescribed drugs in surgeries around the country is the anti-depressant. More and more people are feeling overwhelmed by twentieth-century pressures and concerns, and are afraid that they won't cope. Only today I had a letter from a young lady who seemed to be eaten up by worries and feelings of inadequacy. 'All I seem to do,' she writes, 'is stand helplessly by, watching my life flash past me like a video-tape, while others are surging on in life.'

Now maybe that girl who, as far as I know is a Christian, needs the help of a doctor, for personally I don't believe that Christians are any more immune to being mentally ill than they are from having sore throats or tummy-aches. Nor do I believe that Christians are never prone to 'Monday morning blues'. Of course we're human and still have emotional highs and lows, and ups and downs.

What I do think is that we miss out on taking hold of God's promises and claiming them for ourselves. After all, it's only in the thick of pressures and concerns and difficulties that we would be able to test the promise anyway. It's when we're weak and vulnerable and at our wits' end that we'll prove Him, not when we're feeling self-sufficient and reckon we've everything buttoned up and under control. At those times — when we're doing the coping — we're hardly likely to notice His grace and that's what Paul was getting at when he said, 'When I am weak, then I am strong'.

The grace of God won't make the hard times go away. As far as we can tell, Paul's 'thorn in the flesh' was a permanent drag right through his life, but look how Paul coped — not because he was strong or had great will-power, but because God's power was enough, sufficient for all he had to do.

It's the same for you and me. God's promises don't wear out with time, nor are they selective. They apply to us and this one, as direct and unambiguous as any, guarantees that his grace is all we need. Whatever the problem, whatever the pressure, whatever the hardship, His grace is enough to get us through. It's down to us to believe it and act on it.

DIFFERENT STANDARDS

Now when he saw the crowds, he went up on a mountainside and sat down. His disciples came to him, and he began to teach them, saying:
'Blessed are the poor in spirit,
for theirs is the kingdom of heaven.
Blessed are those who mourn,
for they will be comforted.
Blessed are the meek,
for they will inherit the earth.
Blessed are those who hunger and thirst for righteousness,
for they will be filled.
Blessed are the merciful,
for they will be shown mercy.

Blessed are the pure in heart,
for they will see God.
Blessed are the peacemakers,
for they will be called sons of God.
Blessed are those who are persecuted because of righteousness,
for theirs is the kingdom of heaven.
'Blessed are you when people insult you, persecute you and falsely say all kinds of evil against you because of me. Rejoice and be glad, because great is your reward in heaven, for in the same way they persecuted the prophets who were before you.'

Matthew 5:1-12

On one of these pages I've described the Christian life as 'swimming against the tide'. What I mean is that popular thinking and attitudes are charging off in one direction, while the Christian faith stands solidly for values and priorities that are distinctive and different.

Most of Matthew's famous beatitudes or 'blesseds', for instance, are plain nonsense for a world which doesn't acknowledge God. Whoever heard of the 'poor in spirit' or the 'meek' or the 'persecuted' being society's happy and successful people? (That's what 'blessed' really means!) It's more likely the pushy, the cunning, the ruthless and the thick-skinned. They're the ones who get on in this world and are looked up to and admired. The question is, who's got it right? Whose values are true and more satisfying and whose do we actually observe? Those that the world measures by, or these that mark success in God's kingdom?

There's not the space for a comment on each beatitude, although I know some may need explanation, but don't you know and appreciate, for instance, the peacemakers around us, who, by just 'being there', seem to ease tensions and smooth relationships? And what about the merciful in a world quick to condemn and find fault? Or the 'pure in heart', who stand out so sharply among all those with dubious and mixed motives?

In every generation there are those who are dissatisfied with both the status quo and the direction of current trendy opinion. They want change in society, a system radically different and more honest. Unfortunately, sometimes radical causes become aggressively anti-social and underline the worst in human nature, rather than focus on the best.

My advice is, if it's radical thinking and radical behaviour you're after, then don't look further than the beatitudes. Values like this could turn society upside-down.

ACTIONS SPEAK LOUDER ...

What good is it, my brothers, if a man claims to have faith but has no deeds? Can such faith save him? Suppose a brother or sister is without clothes and daily food. If one of you says to him, 'Go, I wish you well; keep warm and well fed,' but does nothing about his physical needs, what good is it? In the same way, faith by itself, if it is not accompanied by action, is dead.

James 2:14-17

Ever heard the criticism levelled at some Christians that they're 'too heavenly-minded to be any earthly use'? I think it's a rebuke often well deserved, because all too easily our Christian lives get lopsided and, while we're strong on meetings and rallies, we're pretty pathetic at loving our neighbour.

There are some very strong words in the Bible about a Christianity that's all piety and no action, and throughout its history the church has allowed the pendulum to swing from extreme spirituality to extreme 'good works' and then back again. Only rarely has it struck a happy balance between those two equally crucial responsibilities.

It's as though Christianity has dual dimensions. There is the vertical one, which is a person's relationship with God through Jesus. That has to be firm and secure, and is the pillar upon which everything else depends. But there's also the horizontal dimension — our relationship with other people. The Bible makes it clear that Christian commitment is no cop-out from the world and its problems. Quite the reverse. It's an 'opt-in'. And the belief that maintains that being 'right with God' is sufficient in itself is wrong. James is adamant that faith without works is dead. It's mere religiosity — boring and useless.

I go on a lot about my Tear Fund trips to Bangladesh and Africa, I know, but I suppose it's in those missionary situations — in clinics and hospitals, children's homes and workshops — in desperately poor and needy places that I've seen the two dimensions combined to display a love and compassion that speak volumes, not about the missionaries themselves but about their God.

Maybe in the U.K. loving our neighbour has to be more subtle. Perhaps the Welfare State gives us fewer opportunities. All I know is that, when it comes to really selfless caring, we need to pray a little less and do a little more. On second thoughts, perhaps I need to pray a little more and do a whole load more!

WHAT'S IT WORTH?

Jesus sat down opposite the place where the offerings were put and watched the crowd putting their money into the temple treasury. Many rich people threw in large amounts. But a poor widow came and put in two very small copper coins, worth only a fraction of a penny.

Calling his disciples to him, Jesus said, 'I tell you the truth, this poor widow has put more into the treasury than all the others. They all gave out of their wealth; but she, out of her poverty, put in everything — all she had to live on.'

Mark 12:41-44

It isn't what you give, it's why you give it. That's the principle behind the widow's mite and, although it applies directly to our finances, it's just as applicable to our time and energy and talents. Our natural inclination is to compare everything we give to the Lord with what other people give. Is it more or less? Are we up to their expectations? Many of the religious folk in the Temple courts would have looked down their noses at the widow's miserable little offering. It was an insult, they thought. Far from it, according to Jesus. To Him it was worth more than all the other offerings, because it reflected a greater commitment to God. It didn't matter that the amount was small; that wasn't the point. It was the heart behind the gift that gave Him pleasure.

There are two principles in the Bible which govern the Christian's giving — this is one, and it's directed to those who, because of other pressures and responsibilities, have genuinely little to offer. The news for you is that the Lord knows and understands. He doesn't ask for more than you have.

But there's another guideline which, dare I suggest, is relevant to the majority of us. 'To whom much is given,' says Jesus, 'much will be required, for greater is their responsibility.' Relatively speaking, Christians in Britain have 'much given'. Our standard of living is high and, whether you own one television or two, are a one-car family or two, makes little difference. In God's sight, degrees of wealth are not the issue. It's our willingness to let go of what we have got that concerns Him. If Jesus is Lord, then He must be Lord of our pocket money and wages and bank account. That was the problem for the rich young ruler, who is such a vivid contrast to the poor widow. He'd carefully obeyed all the religious rules and regulations, but became 'very sad', says Luke, when Jesus told him to sell what he had and give it to the poor. He so wanted to separate his finance from his faith. In that way, *he* could remain lord of it.

Maybe for you it's something else that gets in the way of Christ's Lordship in your life. Something that you'd love to keep for yourself. If that's so, then consider Jesus' instructions to that wealthy ruler. 'You still lack one thing. Deal with it, then come, follow me.'

WHAT WE WANT, O.K.?

'So now I charge you in the sight of all Israel and of the assembly of the LORD, and in the hearing of our God: Be careful to follow all the commands of the LORD your God, that you may possess this good land and pass it on as an inheritance to your descendants for ever.

'And you, my son Solomon, acknowledge the God of your father, and serve him with wholehearted devotion and with a willing mind, for the LORD searches every heart and understands every motive behind the thoughts. If you seek him, he will be found by you; but if you forsake him, he will reject you for ever. Consider now, for the LORD has chosen you to build a temple as a sanctuary. Be strong and do the work.'

1 Chronicles 28:8-10

It's all wise advice that David passed to his son, but there's one phrase in particular that needled itself into my thinking. It's that Solomon was to have 'a willing mind'. I've been chewing on that — a willing mind.

I've an idea there are a lot of reluctant Christians about. I mean that we've made a general commitment of our lives to Christ, but aren't willing to really step out all the way with Him. We can be hesitant like that and still believe every point of Christian doctrine and possess great understanding of the Bible. We can have a deep and genuine emotional experience of Jesus in our lives. We can even, through a particular set of circumstances — and I'm referring to you older Christians now — be slotted into some specific niche of Christian service or activity, like teaching at Sunday School or serving on a church council. All those things of course are right and good. But it's still possible to remain self-willed — to have given over our minds and hearts to the Lord, but to be holding back with our wills — and, boiled down, that means we do what we want to do, we go where we want to go, we worship how we want to worship, and so on. It's *our* will that rules, O.K., young or old!

Full Christian commitment is being willing for God to do with us whatever He pleases, whatever the personal cost. Are we willing for that? It's a simple question, but the answer determines how much God is able to do with us and for us.

ALL THAT GLITTERS...

'Not everyone who says to me,
"Lord, Lord," will enter the kingdom
of heaven, but only he who does the
will of my Father who is in heaven.
Many will say to me on that day,
"Lord, Lord, did we not prophesy in
your name, and in your name drive
out demons and perform many
miracles?" Then I will tell them
plainly, "I never knew you. Away
from me, you evildoers!"'

Matthew 7:21-23

Grim-sounding words these, and a reminder that Jesus wasn't always gentle,
meek and mild. On occasions He must have sounded downright ferocious.

The key to this stern warning is back in 1 Samuel in the Old Testament,
when the Lord says to Samuel, 'Man looks at the outward appearance but the
Lord looks at the heart.' As a performer, I know how easy it is to act out certain
moods or emotions on stage, when maybe you're feeling very different inside.
That's O.K. on stage — everyone knows that theatre and entertainment is
largely a make-believe world.

In the real world, and particularly in His church, God has no time for play-
actors — a word that really means 'hypocrite'. In Jesus' time, many of the
Pharisees were hypocrites — men who, on the face of it, were tremendously
religious, who observed all the proper religious customs, and who spoke the
right pious jargon, but whose motives and attitudes were anything but godly. In
other words, they were fakes and Jesus knew it.

Over the years, nothing has changed. There are still hypocrites — and God
knows them — but our concern should be to examine ourselves. It's far too easy
to bother about someone else's sincerity.

It's a sobering thought that God not only knows what we do, but why we do
it and, from His viewpoint, the 'why' is more important than the 'what'. As far
as He is concerned, doing religious things and saying religious words are in
themselves totally unimpressive. It's only when they're done and said because
we love Him and want to obey Him that they become not only accepted, but
delight Him into the bargain!

POTTER'S CLAY

*Yet, O LORD, you are our
    Father.
We are the clay, you are the
    potter;
we are all the work of your
    hand.*

*Do not be angry beyond
    measure, O LORD;
do not remember our sins
    for ever.
Oh, look upon us, we pray,
    for we are all your people.*

Isaiah 64:8-9

I guess most of you will be too young to remember those old pieces of film that BBC-TV used to show as interludes when their continuity went up the spout or there was a sudden transmitter collapse. There was one of an aquarium, with fish swimming round and round, looking as bored as the viewers probably felt; and another of a lazy rural scene, with grazing sheep and gently plodding farmers, designed again, I suppose, to soothe frustration. The really memorable sequence, which was fascinating and riveting in its own right, was film of a potter turning his clay on a wheel. All you saw was a close-up of the slippery hands around the wet spinning clay. And, as the skilful fingers and palms exerted just the right pressure here and there, so the clay took on one shape after another, almost as though it had a life of its own. I don't remember whether there was any finished pot or vase. Just as soon as one object seemed to be appearing, a little nudge from the potter's thumb would cause it to merge into something quite different. The artistry was phenomenal and every so often that classic bit of film gets dusted down and brought out for another transmission.

Whenever I see it now, I think of Isaiah's lovely picture of God fashioning His children, moulding them into what He wants them to be, just as a potter would gently and carefully shape his clay. From virtually useless, ugly material, the potter can create something beautiful and worthwhile. Miraculously, from ordinary 'nothing to shout about' lives, God can do just the same. But first there is preparation: before the potter can use it, the clay has to be broken down and thoroughly cleansed and worked on. The analogy still applies. Lives that are unyielding and stubborn and full of imperfection sometimes have to be completely broken down before they can be built up again to be new and useful.

There's a chorus I used to sing with the kids at Bible class that turns the idea into a prayer. 'Thou art the potter, I am the clay; mould me and make me in Thine own way; whatever the vessel, grant me to be fit for Thy service, to glorify Thee.'

START AT HOME

Those who had seen it told the people how the demon-possessed man had been cured. Then all the people of the region of the Gerasenes asked Jesus to leave them, because they were overcome with fear. So he got into the boat and left.

The man from whom the demons had gone out begged to go with him, but Jesus sent him away, saying, 'Return home and tell how much God has done for you.' So the man went away and told all over the town how much Jesus had done for him.

Luke 8:36-39

I don't understand much about demons or evil spirits, although I believe they're a real force right enough. It's the tail end of this story I want to underline, which scotches the silly idea that all people whose lives have been changed by Jesus must uproot from their homes and families and go off to some distant land. For this man, it was exactly the opposite. He was to go home and tell people there what Jesus had done for him.

Sometimes, of course, God does direct otherwise, and a network of missionaries around the world and a growing number of people prepared to share their skills for a year or so in some distant needy area, in the name and for the sake of Jesus, prove it. But, as a rule, Jesus says, 'Stay put. First and foremost, you're to be a witness to me in your own home.' And that's tricky of course, because home is often where it's most difficult. In one sense there's less problem starting from square one where people don't know us and where it's easier to project a new image. At home, with parents, brothers and sisters, it's hard to say, and even harder to show, how much God has done for us. We can't pretend or play games at home. Our folks know us too well. They see us first thing in the morning, when we're grumpy, and they're around when we don't get our own way and tempers flare. There's no way we can fake our Christianity there, that's for sure. But nor is there any way we can duck out of it. If we want to represent Jesus outside our front door, then we must represent Him, first of all, inside.

One of the most beautiful types of letter I'm sent is the one that tells me how a relative at home was a major influence for Jesus. I don't get them often, but I love to hear it. Sometimes a whole family become Christians, one by one, because a brother or sister, or a mum or dad, is faithful and, after being converted, doesn't bottle it up, but shares what Jesus has done in a way that's attractive and convincing.

And it's that last bit that's so important, especially for you young Christians. At home, perhaps more than anywhere else, actions speak louder than words. There's no point in going back home and talking about what Jesus has done for you if you're still bad-tempered and selfish. You can hardly be surprised if the barriers go up! First, your family needs to *see* what He has done for you — then they'll want to hear about it.

A HARD LESSON

After that, he poured water into a basin and began to wash his disciples' feet, drying them with the towel that was wrapped around him.

When he had finished washing their feet, he put on his clothes and returned to his place. 'Do you understand what I have done for you?' he asked them. 'You call me "Teacher" and "Lord", and rightly so, for that is what I am. Now that I, your Lord and Teacher, have washed your feet, you also should wash one another's feet. I have set you an example that you should do as I have done for you.'

John 13:5, 12-15

Here's a hard lesson from Jesus. Washing feet, a routine requirement in those days after long walks on dusty roads in open sandals, was a task reserved for the humblest servant, someone on the very lowest rung of the ladder. Imagine the dismay when Jesus took up the bowl and towel and began to kneel in front of each disciple. After all, this was their leader, their future king, who one day would oust the Romans and give them freedom. How could He stoop so low?

Looking back, we know that Jesus wasn't that kind of political king, but infinitely greater. This was the Son of God washing feet, the same Son of God who commanded the storm to cease, and who cured the sick and crippled. Surely the disciples should have been kneeling before Him!

Why did He do it? Firstly, I think, because He loved so much and was prepared to go to any lengths, no matter how degrading, to show it. And, secondly, to demonstrate the extent that we must go to in loving and caring for one another. That's what I mean by 'a hard lesson'. I can sit back and take any amount of pleasant attention. Sometimes I reckon I've worked hard and have a right to it. Yet here's Jesus, who had rights to everything, washing the disciples' feet.

It's pride of course that's our problem. Pride that keeps us from real sacrificial service, and convinces us that we're a cut above dirtying our hands. We must ask God to rid us of that and give us a little of the readiness that Jesus showed to put aside His rights, to ignore what others might say or think (and how importantly *that* figures in our behaviour!) and to stoop as low as it takes to serve and help our neighbour.

Easy to say, I know, but for the Christian it isn't an option, remember. 'I have set you an example,' says Jesus, 'that you should do as I have done for you.'

SORRY, I DON'T KNOW

Love never fails, But where there are prophecies, they will cease; where there are tongues, they will be stilled; where there is knowledge, it will pass away. For we know in part and we prophesy in part, but when perfection comes, the imperfect disappears. When I was a child, I talked like a child, I thought like a child, I reasoned like a child. When I became a man, I put childish ways behind me.Now we see but a poor reflection; then we shall see face to face. Now I know in part; then I shall know fully, even as I am fully known.

And now these three remain: faith, hope and love. But the greatest of these is love.

1 Corinthians 13:8-13

I've quoted the first half of this famous chapter about love elsewhere in the book, but I couldn't ignore the rest. There's something here that I'm so glad is in the Bible — intelligent justification for saying, 'I don't know'.

As a rule, we don't like admitting to ignorance. It jars at our pride, and saying we don't know can sound a bit like, 'We're not clever enough to understand.' We'd never want people to think that. Actually I don't mind and, when it comes to spiritual matters, issues concerning God and salvation and hell and so on, I reckon that 'I don't know' is sometimes the only honest and valid answer that anyone should give, no matter how great their intelligence or knowledge. Paul states it here clearly enough. There are some matters on which we're not fully informed, not fully in the picture. We have some information but not all. We see an outline but not the detail.

The problems arise when man isn't satisfied with that and wants the mental satisfaction of knowing the lot. That means that what he doesn't and can't know, he makes up and what sounds like authoritative comment is in fact only speculation or theory. It would be harmless enough, I suppose, if the theories didn't cause endless controversy and sometimes bitter disagreements. I'm all for backing away from those grey areas — how God did this; when He'll do that — and owning up to the fact that man's mind is puny and there are things which, quite simply, we don't know.

Let's concentrate faith and study on what we can know and what's been revealed. There's enough there to stretch our minds to the limit anyway. Personally, I'm only too glad to shelve the rest until that time in the future when 'I shall know fully'.

'YOU FEED THEM'

When Jesus landed and saw a large crowd, he had compassion on them and healed their sick.

As evening approached, the disciples came to him and said, 'This is a remote place, and it's already getting late. Send the crowds away, so they can go to the villages and buy themselves some food.'

Jesus replied, 'They do not need to go away. You give them something to eat.'

'We have here only five loaves of bread and two fish,' they answered.

'Bring them here to me,' he said. And he directed the people to sit down on the grass. Taking the five loaves and the two fish and looking up to heaven, he gave thanks and broke the loaves. Then he gave them to the disciples, and the disciples gave them to the people. They all ate and were satisfied, and the disciples picked up twelve basketfuls of broken pieces that were left over. The number of those who ate was about five thousand men, besides women and children.

Matthew 14:14-21

No, you don't ask how it happened. If you believe Jesus had God's power and God's authority and that He was there at the creation of the universe, then the creation of a little food is hardly out of character. The proper question is: does the event teach me anything that's relevant and contemporary? Where is the truth for today? For me, it's two-fold and helps to throw light on the perplexing issue of the world's poor and hungry.

Here Jesus faced a crowd of 5,000 hungry people. There was no shop or market nearby and the only resources were bread and fish which the disciples had with them. It was enough for themselves, no more. But despite that, Jesus' instructions were clear. 'You give them something to eat.' It was their responsibility. Presumably Jesus could have miraculously caused food to appear at the crowd's feet but that wasn't His way. 'You give them something to eat,' He said.

I believe God still gives us the same responsibility. We see the hungry and deprived people of the world, and God says, 'You feed them. You give them medicine. You train them. You care for them.'

And our reaction, like the disciples' at first, is 'What's the point? We have so little.' What was a handful of bread and fish to a crowd of 5,000? It was like passing a 20p bag of peanuts round a packed Hammersmith Odeon! I suppose the disciples could have held back their suppers. It would have been logical to argue that a square meal for twelve was better than a crumb for a hundred. But they didn't hold back. They did as Jesus said and offered what they had. The rest we know. Jesus took their food, blessed it, and used it out of all proportion.

Do you see? The fact that individually our resources are insignificant doesn't matter to God. He can use whatever we let Him have, in ways that we'd never imagine possible. Why do you think so many Christians volunteer their services to help in needy places around the world? Why do thousands give money and time to organisations like Tear Fund? Individually their contributions are relatively pathetic, compared to the vastness of the need. It's because of the conviction that, given to Jesus, those gifts, whatever they are, can be used to achieve miracles. In financial jargon, it's massive return on small investment. What an encouragement to the Christian who thinks he has little to offer by way of finance or personal talent! Just be willing to give Him the little and watch what he does with it.

POWER TO ALL OUR FRIENDS

And what more shall I say? I do not have time to tell about Gideon, Barak, Samson, Jephthah, David, Samuel and the prophets, who through faith conquered kingdoms, administered justice, and gained what was promised; who shut the mouths of lions, quenched the fury of flames, and escaped the edge of the sword; whose weakness was turned to strength; and who became powerful in battle and routed foreign armies.

Hebrews 11:32-34

'All God's giants have been weak men who did great things for God because they reckoned on His being with them.' That was written by the old missionary, Hudson Taylor, and, if you think about it, it's absolutely true. None of the Bible's great characters of faith — some of them are listed here — are supermen. Far from it! Moses, we have already seen, was desperately reluctant to do what God was directing. David seemed pathetically young and inexperienced to be God's champion against Goliath. Nehemiah and friends were called 'those feeble Jews' by their enemies. Jeremiah was scared and overawed by God's call. And the disciples were a motley crew of plain ordinary people — at times, nervous and afraid. Think of Peter, who three times denied he'd ever met Jesus. Sometimes these Bible heroes even did something that was really wrong and shameful — like David, who committed adultery.

Yet, despite their weakness and their vulnerability, God used them — Moses to rescue a multitude of people from Egypt, David to slay a giant and to lead a nation, Nehemiah to rebuild a city, Jeremiah to prophesy to God's people, and the disciples to bring about the greatest revolution the world has ever known. Somehow, as the writer to the Hebrews puts it, their 'weakness was turned to strength.'

It's been the same ever since. God doesn't use people who are different or special or 'super-spiritual'. He chooses ordinary boys and girls and men and women, who believe in Him and who make themselves available to be used in whatever way He wants. It's unlikely, by the way, that you'll be required to shut many mouths of lions!

EQUIPPED FOR BATTLE

Finally, be strong in the Lord and in his mighty power. Put on the full armour of God so that you can take your stand against the devil's schemes. For our struggle is not against flesh and blood, but against the rulers, against the authorities, against the powers of this dark world and against the spiritual forces of evil in the heavenly realms. Therefore put on the full armour of God, so that when the day of evil comes, you may be able to stand your ground, and after you have done everything, to stand. Stand firm then, with the belt of truth buckled around your waist, with the breastplate of righteousness in place, and with your feet fitted with the readiness that comes from the gospel of peace. In addition to all this, take up the shield of faith, with which you can extinguish all the flaming arrows of the evil one. Take the helmet of salvation and the sword of the Spirit, which is the word of God.

Ephesians 6:10-17

It sometimes bothers me when my Christian life gets too cosy and comfortable, because really it never should. There's a war on and Christians have enlisted for front-line service. It's easy, I know, to scoff at the thought of a spiritual battle, but evil forces are attempting to destroy what is good. It sounds kind of weird and old-fashioned. Personally, I don't understand it, but I believe it. I believe it because I'm aware of the struggle in my own life, and I've seen and heard enough to convince me that a supernatural power of evil is just as real and active in our world as God's power of goodness and love. It's a heavy subject but it won't go away by our pretending it doesn't exist.

Tragically, there are some who choose to explore Satan's territory, and suffer the consequences. In my book, anything that even hints of the occult — and that certainly includes ouija boards, glass-tapping, seances and the like — is out. Definitely out — and we're naive and misguided if we think they won't do us harm.

But for the Christian, let's understand that there's nothing to fear. The outcome of the spiritual conflict is already decided. Jesus settled it on the Cross and by rising out of that grave. God's ensured that we're perfectly protected against anything that the Devil might chuck at us. And when testing times come we can be one hundred per cent confident that the armour will be strong enough. Notice that all the pieces are defensive items except one — the sword, which stands for God's Word, the Bible. A sword is for attack and ours is sharp. The more we read our Bible and get to know it, the more we can apply it, and when we do that the Devil is finished.

'Soldiers of Christ, arise, and put your armour on!' Maybe that 'square' old hymn makes sense after all!

AN INNER BATTLE

So I find this law at work: When I want to do good, evil is right there with me. For in my inner being I delight in God's law; but I see another law at work in the members of my body, waging war against the law of my mind and making me a prisoner of the law of sin at work within my members. What a wretched man I am! Who will rescue me from this body of death? Thanks be to God — through Jesus Christ our Lord!

So then, I myself in my mind am a slave to God's law, but in the sinful nature a slave to the law of sin.

Romans 7:21-25

I don't know anyone who doesn't basically understand the difference between right and wrong. It seems to be instinctive in us from the time we're babies. Many people of course can consistently and deliberately ignore or submerge their conscience and choose what is wrong. I guess that, in doing so, they've weighed up the pros and cons and are prepared for the consequences.

But what about those of us who are Christians? We know from the Bible — God's direct word to us — what we should and shouldn't be doing. The standard is spelt out as clear as day, and there's no way we can feign ignorance. Yet, let's face it, time and time again we end up acting contrary to God's wishes, and it's depressing, frustrating, and it can shake our faith.

Here's the other part of that passage that cheers me up no end and gives me hope for the future. Paul — *Saint* Paul, no less — tells us that he had the same problem. That's knowing what was right, wanting to do it deep down in his heart, but somehow failing to come up to the mark. 'I have the desire to do what is good,' he wrote earlier in this chapter, 'but I cannot carry it out.' So what goes wrong? If a Christian has a new nature from God, why does he go on slipping up?

Do you see the answer? There's nothing in the Bible that says God removes our old nature when we become Christians and, as Paul puts it, we have two laws at work inside us, one pulling in one direction, the other in the opposite. As soon as our new nature draws us God's way, our old nature — the old Adam, the Bible describes it — is still there to put a spanner in the works. Even though God amazingly accepts us as perfect through Jesus (I've explained that somewhere else), as soon as we become part of His family, there's no way we really do become sinless either overnight or over a lifetime, come to that. Personally I'm only too aware of my old nature struggling to take control and sometimes succeeding, and I say that to my shame.

If any of this rings bells and you're conscious of a similar warfare, then just fight on. The good news is that potentially your new nature can and will emerge the victor, because Jesus has already won the battle for you. He did that once and for all on the cross. Satan will do his best to tell you otherwise and will use your old self to steer you his way — but Satan's a loser. He may win a round or two, but he won't win the fight. Use your common sense and do all you can to build and feed the new man in you, and similarly do your best to starve and stifle the old one. Again, more of that elsewhere.

Meanwhile, when you lose a round, tell God you're sorry, claim His forgiveness, and go on trusting. And when you want to yell out in despair like Paul, 'Who will rescue me from this body of death?' go back again and again to the historic answer, 'Jesus Christ, our Lord, thanks be to God.'

GROW UP!

Therefore, rid yourselves of all malice and all deceit, hypocrisy, envy, and slander of every kind. Like newborn babies, crave pure spiritual milk, so that by it you may grow up in your salvation, now that you have tasted that the LORD is good.

1 Peter 2:1-3

'For goodness sake, grow up!' If you've been a Christian for a while but wonder why nothing seems to have changed in your life, maybe that's just the advice you need. At the beginning, when we first make our commitment to Jesus, we're like spiritual babies, understanding little and dependent on older, wiser Christians for help and encouragement. It's good that we realise that and not be disillusioned when little seems to happen overnight.

But we're not meant to stay at the milk and nappy stage. There's a point when we have to stand on our own feet and demonstrate signs of spiritual muscle. What does that mean in practice? Firstly, we have to have a regular intake from God's Word, the Bible. That's our spiritual food — our milk — and I know some people who, when they become Christians, seem to develop an enormous appetite. They can't get enough of reading and studying the Bible, and their growth and fast maturity is amazing. Some of us are less ravenous and even the milk is difficult to digest, let alone the meat later on. But we must persevere. Just as milk is crucial to a baby's life, so is the Bible necessary for Christian health. There are all sorts of notes and books written to help you understand it, and your local church, if it is 'alive', is bound to have simple group Bible studies. It's great too to listen to teachers and preachers expounding parts of the Bible. And if you can't get to hear them in person, there are many tape cassettes available of helpful sermons and talks.

Like most analogies, this one breaks down if pushed too far. Babies have bottles placed in their mouths at feeding time by loving mums, but even the youngest Christians have to make some effort themselves to ensure that they're fed. If you've been lazy or uninterested in food, then don't be surprised if your Christian life hasn't taken off. The two go hand in hand. Secondly, don't be a loner. Christians need each other and spiritual hermits — or effective ones anyway — are few and far between. Again it needs discipline and determination, but give time priority to meeting with others in the Christian family. Family get-togethers should be natural and happy occasions, and newborn babies and great-grannies, and all stages in-between, have their place. That's what the church is — a family of God's people and it will nourish and support you, as you gradually flex the muscles.

So come on, baby, grow up and don't be discouraged. A burp or two on the way is only to be expected!

THANK YOU VERY MUCH

Now on his way to Jerusalem, Jesus travelled along the border between Samaria and Galilee. As he was going into a village, ten men who had leprosy met him. They stood at a distance and called out in a loud voice, 'Jesus, Master, have pity on us!'

When he saw them, he said, 'Go, show yourselves to the priests.' And as they went, they were cleansed.

One of them, when he saw he was healed, came back, praising God in a loud voice. He threw himself at Jesus' feet and thanked him — and he was a Samaritan.

Jesus asked, 'Were not all ten cleansed? Where are the other nine? Was no-one found to return and give praise to God except this foreigner?' Then he said to him, 'Rise and go; your faith has made you well.'

Luke 17:11-19

Here is a story about a meeting Jesus had with ten lepers, and it's one that makes me realise I should be showing my thanks to God much more than I do.

You remember that in Jesus' time leprosy was one of the most dreaded illnesses of all because it not only caused a lot of suffering and made faces, hands and feet really ugly and deformed, but it separated people even from their own families and friends. The only folk who would get anywhere near them were other lepers so naturally they went around together, ringing little bells so that healthy people would be warned and could run away. Today leprosy can be quite easily treated with drugs and is no longer the fearful thing it was. Just a few years ago, I remember sitting with a group of leprosy patients at a Christian hospital in Nepal. Although they had scars on their faces and hands, they were happy and getting better after their treatment.

Just imagine how the ten lepers in the story must have felt when they did as Jesus told them and were suddenly well. Never in their wildest dreams could they dare imagine they could ever go back to their homes and families and be normal again. It was the most fantastic thing they could ever have wished for. But it happened — and yet only one came back to Jesus and said thank you.

I wonder what the other nine were doing. Surely they must have *felt* grateful but I guess they were so busy and excited that they forgot to actually *show* their thanks. I know that I — and, I suspect, you as well — have a tremendous amount to thank God for and, although we might sometimes feel glad, Jesus obviously wants more than just a feeling. He wants us to show our gratitude by the way we live our lives.

NO MORE CRYING

'Do not let your hearts be troubled. Trust in God; trust also in me. In my Father's house are many rooms; if it were not so, I would have told you. I am going there to prepare a place for you. And if I go and prepare a place for you, I will come back and take you to be with me that you also may be where I am. You know the way to the place where I am going.'

Thomas said to him, 'Lord, we don't know where you are going, so how can we know the way?'

Jesus answered, 'I am the way and the truth and the life. No-one comes to the Father except through me.'

I saw the Holy City, the new Jerusalem, coming down out of heaven from God, prepared as a bride beautifully dressed for her husband. And I heard a loud voice from the throne saying, 'Now the dwelling of God is with men, and he will live with them. They will be his people, and God himself will be with them and be their God. He will wipe every tear from their eyes. There will be no more death or mourning or crying or pain, for the old order of things has passed away.'

He who was seated on the throne said, 'I am making everything new!' Then he said, 'Write this down, for these words are trustworthy and true.'

John 14:1-6; Revelation 21:2-5

'It's all pie in the sky when you die.' I guess you've heard that one too! The idea that Christianity is merely some convenient insurance policy to wrap around ourselves just in case there's an after-life! I don't know who invents them, but again someone's got hold of the wrong end of the stick. Proportionately, only a small amount of Bible space is given over to what happens when we die and the over-all emphasis is very much on the here and now. The Christian life starts from the moment we commit ourselves to Jesus and it's about the nitty-gritty business of how we get on with other people and what we do with our lives.

But let's get the balance right. Of course a part of the Christian faith — a very important part — does give hope for the future. What marvellous, fantastic prospects there are as far as the Christian is concerned. I'm too busy living my life today to be preoccupied with tomorrow but I'd be some sort of a robot if my emotions weren't churned with excitement at the prospect of a future that Jesus says He has personally prepared for us, and where there's 'no more death or mourning or crying or pain'. Maybe I'm sentimental, but that brings a lump to my throat. At the moment, none of us is immune from suffering. Often tragedy and pain are things which happen to other people but, at some point, they intrude into our homes and lives. Maybe we lose someone we love dearly and it seems as though part of our life has crumbled away. It's at times like these, when we're heartbroken and feel that the future has nothing to offer, that these promises in John and Revelation are such an enormous comfort, because they tell us that sorrow and death aren't the end of the story. There's another perspective, a wider view, that makes grief and loneliness more tolerable, and makes it possible to discover joy in the midst of suffering.

AN ESCAPE ROUTE

If you think you are standing firm, be careful that you don't fall! No temptation has seized you except what is common to man. And God is faithful; he will not let you be tempted beyond what you can bear. But when you are tempted, he will also provide a way out so that you can stand up under it.

1 Corinthians 10:12-13

There's so much of relevance and importance packed into the Bible that sometimes it's wise to focus on just a sentence or two. In these two short verses, there's a warning to the confident and a monster dose of encouragement to those who are anything but.

The warning is simple and aimed at Christians who reckon they're living the Christian life pretty well. Sin is a thing of the past, temptation presents no great problem and, what with all the church Bible studies and prayer meetings, the devil doesn't get a look-in. Wrong thinking. When we reckon we've got it all sewn up, then that's the time to beware, says Paul. All of us, no matter how mature and experienced Christians we may be, are vulnerable, and the greater our confidence in our ability to stand firm, the greater our likely complacency, and the greater our probable fall. Never think that there's some evil which you aren't capable of performing. Certainly there are some things which I can't imagine myself doing, but, at the same time, I know the potential is in me and that 'there, but for the grace of God, go I'.

More common, I suspect, is the exact opposite. The feeling that, as Christians, we're a dead loss. Some recurring failure bugs us again and again, and the more we try to get the better of it, the more it seems to undermine our Christian life. We know we're letting the Lord down, and that just makes it a whole load worse. Maybe it's a lousy temper, a non-helpful relationship, personal pride, whatever — we know what we ought to do and ought not to do, but that same old problem constantly haunts and defeats us.

If that's you, then I'll share a secret — it's me too. In fact you're not one scrap different from all other Christians who are attacked by the devil at the weakest spot in their character. We may think that our Achilles heel is unique, that no-one else could possibly experience the same hassles. Wrong again. There's nothing that you battle with that doesn't trouble millions of others as well. As Paul says, the wrong desires that come into your life aren't anything new and different. That's a comfort in itself — to know that you're not alone. What follows is even better — that no problem need actually be permanent or impossible to cope with. God just doesn't allow it. Sure, He allows the devil to tempt. There's nothing to say we'll be free of that, but at the same time He provides an escape route. Our responsibility is to find it and use it. Personally I'm still learning but the way, I know, is there, and the spiritual resources to help are vast. Just to have that at the back of your mind is a fantastic remedy for despair!

CONFIDENT FAITH

Therefore, since we have a great high priest who has gone through the heavens, Jesus the Son of God, let us hold firmly to the faith we profess. For we do not have a high priest who is unable to sympathise with our weaknesses, but we have one who has been tempted in every way, just as we are — yet was without sin. Let us then approach the throne of grace with confidence, so that we may receive mercy and find grace to help us in our time of need.

Hebrews 4:14-16

'The trouble with the vicar is that he wouldn't understand.' I wonder how often that's been said. Sad really, because the chances are that he'd understand more than you think. This section from the difficult book of Hebrews isn't about the vicar but about Jesus who, in a sense, is our heavenly high priest — the person through whom we can make actual contact with God, our Father. That's why we pray 'in the name of Jesus' and often end our prayers 'through Jesus Christ, our Lord'.

In Old Testament times, the high priest was the man who spoke to God on behalf of the Jews. He was the one who offered all the main sacrifices and who pleaded for the people's forgiveness when they disobeyed. If someone needed to get right with God, he could only do it by going to the high priest, who was the one and only route.

Then Jesus came and did away with all that. No more need for an earthly high priest, bishop or vicar to act as a go-between, because Jesus took over that role. Right now, incredible though it sounds, Jesus is acting as your representative and mine before God. No more sacrifices are needed to put things right, because His own sacrifice on the cross was sufficient for everyone for all time.

I suppose we do sometimes have to pluck up courage to talk to the vicar. Those dog-collars can put you off, but with Jesus it's different. He not only understands our problems, but actually sympathises with us — not because He's done what we've done, but because He's been through our temptation and knows our weakness.

For me, this passage contains one of the most fantastic phrases in all of the Bible. It's those two little words 'with confidence'. Despite what I am, despite all my wickedness, despite all my pathetic failures, I can approach God 'with confidence' because Jesus, my 'high priest', is there to make Cliff Richard acceptable.

As I've said before in this book, if that's not something to get excited about, I give up!

WHO'S YOUR BOSS?

Therefore, as God's chosen people, holy and dearly loved, clothe yourselves with compassion, kindness, humility, gentleness and patience. Bear with each other and forgive whatever grievances you may have against one another. Forgive as the Lord forgave you. And over all these virtues put on love, which binds them all together in perfect unity.

Whatever you do, work at it with all your heart, as working for the Lord, not for men, since you know that you will receive an inheritance from the Lord as a reward. It is the Lord Christ you are serving.

Colossians 3:12-14, 23-24

Should I or shouldn't I — that is the question. Is it right or is it wrong? Am I doing God's will or am I satisfying mine? If you aren't really sure, then apply Paul's test. It's well-nigh infallible. Simply ask, 'Can I really do it for the Lord? Would it please Him?' Your conscience will tell you the answer — the rest is up to you!

I wonder what effect it would have if that verse were hung up in every factory and office around the country. 'Whatever you do, work at it with all your heart, as working for the Lord, not for man.' It would produce a few embarrassed coughs in industry, that's for sure, and notice that all-embracing phrase '*Whatever* you do'. Not just religious things but everything — sport and hobbies, study and training, making friends and making tea. Everything we turn our hand to should be the very best because we're offering it to God and He deserves and demands nothing less. In a sense, as we do that, as we 'do everything as unto the Lord' (as an older version of the Bible puts it), it becomes an act of worship. In that fantastic film 'Chariots of Fire', Eric Liddell, the Olympic athlete, says, 'God made me fast, and when I run I feel His pleasure'.

I promise you, I'm ambitious. I want to hit the top of the charts as often as I can, with the best material I can find, but I want to do it so that God can have the applause. On stage I'm conscious, very conscious, of my audience, but I'm also working for the Lord, and that's the biggest incentive I could ever have for maximum performance. I've been asked whether becoming a Christian helped my career. I'm not sure, but I'm positive it's made me a better singer — just as a Christian perspective must make you a better housewife or butcher or businessman or student.

Try working for Him. The Lord will be delighted — so will your boss!

WHEN GOD DIDN'T LISTEN

*I hate, I despise your religious
    feasts;*
I cannot stand your assemblies.
*Even though you bring me burnt
    offerings and grain offerings,*
I will not accept them.
*Though you bring choice fellowship
    offerings,*
I will have no regard for them.
Away with the noise of your songs!
*   I will not listen to the music of
your harps.*
But let justice roll on like a river,
*   righteousness like a never-failing
stream!*

Amos 5:21-24

Here's another heavy reminder that our attitudes to other people matter more to God than a basinful of church services. Amos was one of those Old Testament prophets who looked at what was going on around him and hated what he saw. Outwardly everything was so religious. The synagogues were full, with sacrifices being offered just as Jewish law demanded. Hymns were being sung and prayers were being chanted nineteen to the dozen. Any visitor would have been knocked out by the piety of it all. Yet to God, Amos says, it didn't mean a light. It was like whistling in the wind. God heard nothing.

You'll need to read more about Amos to understand why. It wasn't that God no longer wanted 'solemn assemblies', worship, sacrifice and singing. He did, but He wanted them from people whose hearts were right and who were living lovingly both towards Him and towards their neighbours. Sadly, many of the religious people of Amos's day were doing anything but. Their society was corrupt and unjust. The rich were getting richer at the expense of the poor, and the weak were exploited and trodden on by the powerful. Principles of equality and social concern had been abandoned and 'Blow you, I'm all right, Joshua!' was fast becoming the prevalent attitude.

And Amos could stand and watch the hypocrisy of it no longer. For him it was first things first. When people were living justly with their neighbour and were at least attempting to reflect a little of God's righteousness, then, and only then, could they call upon the Lord and expect His blessing.

It occurs to me, as I am sure it does to you, that, as we look around our world today and see the contrasts of living standards, opportunities and privileges, and the apparent nonchalance and complacency that exist about us, Amos might well have a similar word for Christians in the Eighties. I guess he'd not be too polite about it either!

A PERMANENT PARTNERSHIP

Then the eleven disciples went to Galilee, to the mountain where Jesus had told them to go. When they saw him, they worshipped him; but some doubted. Then Jesus came to them and said, 'All authority in heaven and on earth has been given to me. Therefore go and make disciples of all nations, baptising them in the name of the Father and of the Son and of the Holy Spirit, and teaching them to obey everything I have commanded you. And surely I will be with you always, to the very end of the age.'

Matthew 28:16-20

People seem surprised that, after all these years, I still get petrified before facing an audience. It isn't as bad now as it used to be. In the early days I got physically sick before going on stage. Now it's just a dry mouth and a stomach full of butterflies! I guess that, if you multiply that sensation a few hundred times, you'll get an idea how the disciples must have felt when Jesus left them. His work on earth was done and He was about to return to the Father and to His rightful place. Now the responsibility rested on the disciples. It was up to them to share what they had seen and heard and understood. If they kept quiet and said nothing, Christianity would fizzle out almost before it began — but that wasn't God's intention.

Those disciples were very human. Even after three years with Jesus, after seeing His miracles, hearing His teaching, receiving His love — some, Matthew tells us, still doubted. After all that, they still weren't sure.

To be fair, maybe their doubts weren't about Jesus Himself. After all that had happened, they must have been convinced about Him. Perhaps they were more nervous about their own ability to carry on without Him. That I *can* understand. Always Jesus had been right there to advise and direct and encourage. Now they were out in the big wide world on their own — or so they thought. Obviously they hadn't anticipated one last promise: 'I will be with you always, to the very end of the age.'

As though Jesus would have left His followers with an impossible task! On their own of course it would have been impossible — and you and I would certainly be in very different circumstances today if that little gang of eleven men had been abandoned to their own devices. But, by His Spirit, Jesus stayed with them — even lived in them — to transform their lives and continue his work.

That was nearly two thousand years ago yet, in one sense, nothing has changed. Jesus' followers still have a responsibility to make Him known to others. Many of us still doubt whether we really can, only to discover that the promise still stands and, in a supernatural way, impossible to analyse scientifically, Jesus somehow shares His life and His resources with us, so that you and I, and Christians all over the world, can be used to introduce others to Jesus, so that they too are baptised in the name of the Father and of the Son and of the Holy Spirit.

CONSTANTLY

Who shall separate us from the love of Christ? Shall trouble or hardship or persecution or famine or nakedness or danger or sword? As it is written:
'For your sake we face death all
  day long;
  we are considered as sheep to
  be slaughtered.'
No, in all these things we are more than conquerors through him who loved us. For I am convinced that neither death nor life, neither angels nor demons, neither the present nor the future, nor any powers, neither height nor depth, nor anything else in all creation, will be able to separate us from the love of God that is in Christ Jesus our Lord.

Romans 8:35-39

My Bible virtually falls open by itself at this page. And I guess I'd choose these particular verses as the most reassuring, encouraging, and out-and-out fantastic in the whole of Scripture. How can you be unmoved by news that God loves you like this? That there's nowhere you or I can go, nowhere we can slink away to or hide that outdistances us from God's love. Nothing we can do will put us beyond it, no-one and nothing can get in the way and obstruct it. Uninterrupted, constant, outgoing love from God to me, from God to you.

It's hard to grasp because human love is all we have to compare it to. And although wonderful where it exists, human love is fallible. Even love of parent for child sometimes breaks down and confidence is shattered and scars are permanent. Love between husband and wife can dim, and relationships that begin so beautifully and with such apparent commitment can end in hurt and separation.

Personally, I don't know of any love that even approaches the one described here, for it demands absolutely nothing in return and is one hundred per cent unconditional. Break His law and His love is none the less. Misuse His name as angry swear-words and His love is the same. Live a life that denies His very existence and His love will pursue you to the last moment.

Countless numbers of people have been drawn to Christ and to Christian commitment simply by catching sight of that love. Intellectual arguments have suddenly seemed irrelevant. Uncertainties about the future and where God might lead have gone by the board. The love of Jesus, unshakeable and certain, is irresistible. And may I say that, if anyone reading this book has never personally welcomed or maybe never appreciated or understood that love before, please respond to it.

There's nothing I can add. Just read the passage again.

MAKE YOUR MIND UP TIME

So Ahab sent word throughout all Israel and assembled the prophets on Mount Carmel. Elijah went before the people and said, 'How long will you waver between two opinions? If the LORD is God, follow him; but if Baal is God, follow him.'

At the time of sacrifice, the prophet Elijah stepped forward and prayed: 'O LORD, God of Abraham, Isaac and Israel, let it be known today that you are God in Israel and that I am your servant and have done all these things at your command. Answer me, O LORD, answer me, so these people will know that you, O LORD, are God, and that you are turning their hearts back again.'

Then the fire of the LORD fell and burned up the sacrifice, the wood, the stones and the soil, and also licked up the water in the trench.

When all the people saw this, they fell prostrate and cried, 'The LORD, he is God! The LORD — he is God!'

1 Kings 18:20-21, 36-39

They seem really hard men, those Old Testament prophets! No pussy-footing around — straight in with two feet. In today's society I guess they wouldn't be too welcome — not that they were all that popular in their own day, come to that. 'Intolerant, too dogmatic, insensitive' — you can imagine the reaction.

Yet for me Elijah's directness is tremendous and, for my money, there's too little of it around. Of course it's right to have respect for others and their opinions, but there are occasions when it's 'make-your-mind-up-time' and the dithering has to stop. Occasions when we should be saying, 'O.K., you've been considering the claims of Jesus long enough. Now it's time for a decision — you're either for Him or against Him.'

Dylan's song 'You Gotta Serve Somebody' hits the nail on the head. If it isn't the Lord you're serving, it might be wise to ask yourself just who or what it is.

THE MAKER'S RULES

'I am the LORD your God, who brought you out of Egypt, out of the land of slavery.

'You shall have no other gods before me.

'You shall not make for yourself an idol in the form of anything in heaven above or on the earth beneath or in the waters below. You shall not bow down to them or worship them; for I, the LORD your God, am a jealous God, punishing the children for the sin of the fathers to the third and fourth generation of those who hate me, but showing love to thousands who love me and keep my commandments.

'You shall not misuse the name of the LORD your God, for the LORD will not hold anyone guiltless who misuses his name.

'Observe the Sabbath day by keeping it holy, as the LORD your God has commanded you. Six days you shall labour and do all your work, but the seventh day is a Sabbath to the LORD your God. On it you shall not do any work, neither you, nor your son or daughter, nor your manservant or maidservant, nor your ox,

---

I reckon I'd make a good dad because, as well as loving my kids, I'd be firm with them. I honestly don't believe that a 'do as you like' approach to life actually works. It sounds all very well, and the button badges all recommend 'If it feels good, do it'. But I am convinced that that's bad advice. All of us, no matter what age we are, need reliable ground rules for living — some basic guidelines, if you like, to help us live life happily and successfully.

If I buy a new car, I expect to be told by the maker how to use it properly. There will be certain rules. Of course, I could ignore them: I could put oil in the petrol tank and petrol in the oil sump if I wanted to. It's my car and I can do what I like with it. But if I do, it's no use me complaining to the maker; he'll simply say, 'It was your choice, I told you what was right.'

I have heard people say that the Ten Commandments are outdated and

your donkey or any of
your animals, nor the
alien within your gates,
so that your manservant
and maidservant may
rest, as you do.
Remember that you
were slaves in Egypt and
that the LORD your God
brought you out of there
with a mighty hand and
an outstretched arm.
Therefore the LORD your
God has commanded you
to observe the Sabbath
day.
'Honour your father and your
mother, as the LORD your
God has commanded
you, so that you may live
long and that it may go
well with you in the land
the LORD your God is
giving you.
'You shall not murder.
'You shall not commit
adultery.
'You shall not steal.
'You shall not give false
testimony against your
neighbour.
'You shall not covet your
neighbour's wife. You
shall not set your desire
on your neighbour's
house or land, his
manservant or
maidservant, his ox or
donkey, or anything that
belongs to your
neighbour.'

Deuteronomy 5:6-21

---

that being a Christian is merely trying to obey a set of kill-joy rules — you mustn't do this and you mustn't do that. It isn't like that at all. Being a Christian broadens, not cramps, your life — but we do need basic rules and, if you think they're all just negative, then I know full well that, if someone was trying to kill me, Commandment Number 6, for instance, would immediately become very positive from my point of view!

There isn't space for a comment on all ten commandments, but read them through again and ask yourself if, at the root of each one, there isn't plain common sense. Personally, I'd expect the Maker to know what's best and I'd expect a father who loves his children not only to give sensible rules but to require them to be obeyed.

TIME IN BETWEEN

At that time the sign of the Son of Man will appear in the sky, and all the nations of the earth will mourn. They will see the Son of Man coming on the clouds of the sky, with power and great glory, And he will send his angels with a loud trumpet call, and they will gather his elect from the four winds, from one end of the heavens to the other.

Therefore keep watch, because you do not know on what day your Lord will come. But understand this: If the owner of the house had known at what time of night the thief was coming, he would have kept watch and would not have let his house be broken into. So you also must be ready, because the Son of Man will come at an hour when you do not expect him.

Matthew 24:30-31, 42-44

If we believe that Jesus, God's Son, was here on earth once, it doesn't strike me as far-fetched or improbable that one day He will be back. God had a plan for the beginning of the world and He has a plan for its end. We don't know the details, but Jesus left no room for doubt about the principle.

Some day He will return. Not this time unnoticed as a helpless baby in a remote Middle Eastern village, but as Lord and ultimate Judge of everyone who has ever lived. Don't ask me how. My mind can't grasp the mechanics of it. I just know that, when it happens, there will be no dispute or controversy about whether it is or isn't Jesus. Everyone will know and everyone, according to the Bible, will be bowing before Him — some, I presume, in dismay, others in love and worship.

The second coming of Jesus is a massive subject and there's no way I could explain it in a whole book, let alone in a few paragraphs. But here are three basic truths, as I understand them.

(1) When Jesus comes it will mark the end of the world as we know it. Christians hold different interpretations about what form the new order will take. As for me, I'd rather not speculate. What I am sure about is that the world won't be blown to smithereens, beyond God's control, through some nuclear madness. God is sovereign. He is in control and nothing will interfere with that last chapter of history. I'm just relieved that God's written it, and not man.

(2) You and I and everyone who has ever lived must stand before Jesus for His judgement. For some, that could be a terrifying prospect — but only if they've rejected or neglected God's forgiveness. I've written about that elsewhere. For those who know their sin has been dealt with and wiped out, that encounter with Jesus is something to anticipate with total confidence and excitement.

(3) Jesus will come when we're not expecting Him. Ignore all those people who predict a certain date or a certain year. History is littered with predictions like that; all of them proved futile and time-wasting. The Bible says His coming will be like a thief in the night — and a thief doesn't exactly mail you a note to say he's on his way! In other words, He'll come suddenly and unexpectedly. For sure, we have a good basis for thinking that arrival time may not be far off — again, more about that in another section — but the actual time we don't know.

Meanwhile, the wisest and most logical advice is to live as though it could be today. In the words of Larry Norman's song: 'I wish we'd all been ready'.

WEAK AND WOBBLY

After the death of Moses the servant of the LORD, the LORD said to Joshua son of Nun, Moses' assistant: 'Moses my servant is dead. Now then, you and all these people, get ready to cross the Jordan River into the land I am about to give to them — to the Israelites. I will give you every place where you set your foot, as I promised Moses. Your territory will extend from the desert and from Lebanon to the great river, the Euphrates — all the Hittite country — and to the Great Sea on the west. No-one will be able to stand up against you all the days of your life. As I was with Moses, so I will be with you; I will never leave you or forsake you.

'Be strong and courageous, because you will lead these people to inherit the land I swore to their forefathers to give them. Be strong and very courageous. Be careful to obey all the law my servant Moses gave you; do not turn from it to the right or to the left, that you may be successful wherever you go. Do not let this Book of the Law depart from your mouth; meditate on it day and night, so that you may be careful to do everything written in it. Then you will be prosperous and successful. Have I not commanded you? Be strong and courageous. Do not be terrified; do not be discouraged, for the LORD your God will be with you wherever you go.'

Joshua 1:1-9

Here's another instance of someone facing up to a new challenge and finding strength and encouragement from God. This time it's Joshua, feeling all weak and wobbly at the knees when he has to take over from Moses as leader of the Israelites. The responsibility is huge and the task is dangerous and daunting. Any normal person would feel scared and inadequate, and the fact that Moses had created such a massive impression before him wasn't exactly helpful. Just think what he had to live up to!

This time God's promise to Joshua is conditional. Certainly God would give him strength and success. Certainly God would be with him, just as He was with Moses (that must have been some relief!). But it was dependent on Joshua being absolutely obedient to God's Word. He couldn't expect God to bless him if he ignored instructions. This was the key — knowing and following the guidelines.

And, all these thousands of years afterwards, that's still the key. Maybe we don't have such a massive task as Joshua had, but all of us want to make a success of our lives — real success, I mean, which brings peace and fulfilment — and God says that can happen, but only if we keep to the guidelines. And that's not easy unless we know what the guidelines are. Joshua's 'Bible' wasn't very big — just one book of the law, handed down from Moses. Ours is much larger and more involved, but the principle is unchanged — study it, obey it, add a pinch of trust and an ounce of courage, and you have the recipe for prosperity and success.

And if that's not incentive enough, read the last sentence again. 'For remember, the Lord your God will be with you wherever you go.' What more can I ask?

CAN I BE SURE?

And this is the testimony: God has given us eternal life, and this life is in his Son. He who has the Son has life; he who does not have the Son of God does not have life.

I write these things to you who believe in the name of the Son of God so that you may know that you have eternal life. This is the assurance we have in approaching God: that if we ask anything according to his will, he hears us. And if we know that he hears us — whatever we ask — we know that we have what we asked of him.

1 John 5:11-15

'You're too dogmatic,' people have said. 'How can you be so sure you're right?' I must remember to quote this little section when I next hear that, because of course I'm only dogmatic because the Bible's dogmatic. There are only two categories of people, according to John—those who have Jesus and therefore have life, and those who don't have Jesus and who are missing out. No in-betweens, no shades of grey: you're either a have or a have-not. You're either in the family or out of it. Now that's dogmatic—it's also clear and leaves no room for doubt. It was the same with Jesus. There were sheep or goats, according to Him; righteous or unrighteous; lost or found. Again, no category for the 'don't knows'.

And that's the other thing. It isn't presumptuous to say 'I know I'm a Christian,' because the Bible says we can and should be certain. 'I write these things', says John, 'so that you may *know* that you have eternal life'. Not that you may 'hope' you have it, or 'think you might', but that you may *know*. And if that still sounds presumptuous to you, it's possibly because you think that claiming to be a Christian is a bit like blowing your own trumpet and implying that your life is that much better than the next guy's. That's one of those awful but popular misunderstandings. The point is that Christians have no trumpet whatsoever of their own to blow. The fact that I'm a Christian doesn't make me even a gnat better than the non-Christian right next to me. And, if it were down to me to qualify for eternal life by achieving some level of goodness, then forget it. Thank heavens it isn't down to me but it's down to Jesus! That's why it isn't presumptuous to 'know', because faith rests not on me or what I do but entirely on who Jesus is and what He has done. I'm a Christian solely because Jesus, the Son of God, died in my place so that I need not fear death, and now, by His Spirit, lives in my life so I can enjoy it to the full.

Have a think about that stark dividing line. As far as God is concerned, if you don't have Jesus, you haven't begun to live.

A GRIM ALTERNATIVE

We must pay more careful attention, therefore, to what we have heard, so that we do not drift away. For if the message spoken by angels was binding, and every violation and disobedience received its just punishment, how shall we escape if we ignore such a great salvation? This salvation, which was first announced by the LORD, was confirmed to us by those who heard him. God also testified to it by signs, wonders and various miracles, and gifts of the Holy Spirit distributed according to his will.

Hebrews 2:1-4

Some of those old fire-and-brimstone preachers of our great-grandad's day must have been terrifying characters, with all their ranting and raving and talk about hellfire and damnation. No wonder they had their congregations knocking at the knees! It's not for me, that sort of emphasis, because it isn't the Bible's emphasis. The recurring theme of Scripture is God's mercy and His longing to forgive and restore.

But hold on a minute! Whether we like it or not, or whether it's fashionable or not, there's one very definite strand of teaching in the Bible that isn't so palatable. It isn't prominent but it's there, and we can't pick and choose what we'll believe just because it suits us. It's all or nothing. The short of it is that those who have had the opportunity to receive Jesus as Lord and Saviour and have chosen either to reject Him and go it alone, or have simply chosen to do nothing, face the consequences of an eternity separated from God.

I don't know what that means, any more than I can grasp what heaven will be like. All I do appreciate is that to be with God for ever will be fantastic; to be cut off from Him for ever will be appalling and uncomfortable and it's what Scripture calls hell. For the Christian, hell has ceased to be an option. Through Jesus, God has fixed our ultimate destination and that's irrevocable. Nothing, but nothing, can change that.

But for the person reading this who isn't a Christian, I wouldn't dare elaborate — other than to repeat what must be the Bible's most chilling question: 'How shall we escape if we ignore such a great salvation?' Neglect — not turn our back in anger, rebellion or disagreement. A few do that but not many. For the vast majority it is just neglect. Jesus is around somewhere, like the old trunks and packing-cases in the attic that haven't been disturbed for years.

Personally, I believe that you neglect Jesus at your peril. Please consider it well.

FAKES AND CHARLATANS

As Jesus was sitting on the Mount of Olives, the disciples came to him privately. 'Tell us,' they said, 'when will this happen, and what will be the sign of your coming and of the end of the age?'

Jesus answered: 'Watch out that no-one deceives you. For many will come in my name, claiming, "I am the Christ," and will deceive many. You will hear of wars and rumours of wars, but see to it that you are not alarmed. Such things must happen, but the end is still to come. Nation will rise against nation, and kingdom against kingdom. There will be famines and earthquakes in various places. All these are the beginning of birth-pains.'

Matthew 24:3-8

The more you delve into the subject of Jesus' second coming, the more intriguing it is. And if you were to list all the Bible's predictions about what must occur first — and there are a surprising number of quite detailed predictions — you'd be amazed how many have already come true. Only a few are left to be fulfilled, and I don't think it's being dramatic or sensational therefore to regard the great climax of history — the King's arrival — to be within a relatively short span of time. There's little doubt that the 'false Christs' mentioned here are emerging from all sorts of holes in the woodwork. Just recently, someone or some group spent thousands of pounds on full-page advertisements in the world's press, announcing that the Messiah was here and would be declaring his presence on a certain date in a certain town. Needless to say, the date came and went and no-one declared anything of much world importance. Just imagine those red faces!

What nonsense all that sort of talk is. It's good to beware of those groups and systems, churches and 'personalities', who spring up seemingly overnight (often from America!) and claim to have a special revelation of the truth. Jesus said, 'Follow me'. No structure or philosophy, just 'me'.

But we shouldn't be surprised that bizarre sects and cults attract. Jesus said they would. Similarly, He predicted wars and rumours of wars, and increasing natural calamities. He wasn't a scaremonger, nor are those who repeat His warnings. For the Christian, the future isn't scary. Quite the opposite. I love that phrase in the Anglican prayer-book about Christians having a 'sure and certain hope'. I'm looking forward to that day and whether it's in my lifetime or not doesn't really matter. I just hope we'll meet at the celebration!

STRAIGHT FROM THE SHOULDER

Then he said to them all: 'If anyone would come after me, he must deny himself and take up his cross daily and follow me. For whoever wants to save his life will lose it, but whoever loses his life for me will save it. What good is it for a man to gain the whole world, and yet lose or forfeit his very self? If anyone is ashamed of me and my words, the Son of Man will be ashamed of him when he comes in his glory and in the glory of the Father and of the holy angels.'

Luke 9:23-26

I've written a great deal in these pages about the benefits of the Christian life. Quite right too, because there are many, and I wouldn't swop my years as a Christian for any number in the crowded spiritual wilderness. But listen — don't approach Christianity with the idea that it's all get and no give, like some big permanent hand-out. It's neither a hand-out, nor an easy formula for ironing out life's wrinkles.

Being a Christian is costly. It requires discipline and demands commitment, and if they're offputting words then so it has to be. We must be under no false impressions and, I repeat, if you come to Jesus thinking you're in for an easy ride and a cushy number, then you've misunderstood and should go back to square one. Jesus dangled no carrots and was never guilty of false pretences. His message to would-be followers was uncompromising: 'It will cost you'. Not once does He suggest that discipleship is comfortable or convenient, and His warning here about self-denial and being prepared to 'take up the cross daily' is hardly a winsome commercial. In those days, anyone who carried a cross was en route to execution and the message was plain. 'If you follow me,' Jesus was saying, 'you must be prepared to die.'

O.K., so today being a Christian doesn't as a rule put your life at risk, not physically, but the principle is the same and we have to weigh up very seriously whether it's real Christian commitment we're into, or the innocuous game of Sunday make-believe.

I don't know what the cost of Christian discipleship would be for you. Our circumstances and situations vary, but following Jesus is never easy and you can be sure that, whatever your walk of life, you'll be swimming against the tide, and that in itself is a pressure. You'll need courage and determination to be a Christian, as well as trust and obedience. Sometimes you'll experience a clash of loyalties or a conflict of priorities, and each time Jesus will demand first place, and part of you won't want Him to have it. Yet He never settles for less. Sometimes you'll ask whether it's worth it. The time and effort, the misunderstanding of friends, and even the loss of them. Does Jesus warrant that total commitment and unswerving allegiance? He does for me, but you must make your own decision. Don't be short-sighted, that's all. And remember Jesus' broader view: 'What good is it for a man to gain the whole world and yet lose his very self?'

A KEY QUESTION

Jesus and his disciples went on to the villages around Caesarea Philippi. On the way he asked them, 'Who do people say I am?'

They replied, 'Some say John the Baptist; others say Elijah; and still others, one of the prophets.'

'But what about you?' he asked. 'Who do you say I am?'

Peter answered, 'You are the Christ.'

Mark 8:27-29

I've deliberately chosen this to end with, because of Jesus' last question. I guess there must have been a good deal of chat among the disciples about what people were thinking and about the various rumours that were flying. Some of the speculation about Jesus' identity was amazing and sounds like early Fleet Street invention!

Of course, the opinions and ideas of other people are interesting and there's a time to consider them. But suddenly Jesus broke into the discussion with a question that must have stopped them dead in their tracks. 'O.K.,' said Jesus, 'you've heard what others are saying, but what about you? Who do you say I am?' Only Peter answered, and I wonder if at this stage there were a few embarrassed coughs and a bit of foot-shuffling from the others.

My book has been self-indulgent and I've told you what I think. They're my views, my opinions, my understandings. You might or might not have found them interesting. But, in the final analysis, they're not vital as far as you are concerned. For me they are, but not for you, because what I think won't determine your relationship with God.

The title of the book is *You, Me and Jesus*. At the end of it, let the focus just be on *You and Jesus*. 'Right,' He says, 'You've read it through. You know what Cliff thinks. But now, what about you? Who do you say I am?'

If you're honest and follow through the implications, your life will be determined by your answer.

SUBJECT INDEX

GOD

His greatness	Psalm 8:1-5	50
	Psalm 62:1-8	44
	Psalm 95:1-7	26
His love	Matthew 6:25-34	68
	Matthew 22:34-40	91
	John 3:13-17	51
	Romans 8:35-39	138
His plan to save us	John 19:28-30	73
	Acts 16:25-34	80
	1 Timothy 1:15-17	27
His goodness	Luke 15:25-32	70
His faithfulness	Psalm 139:1-10	111
	Romans 8:28-30	23
	2 Corinthians 12:7-10	112
His justice	Joshua 7:20-25	32
	Hebrews 2:1-4	147
His enabling	Exodus 3:10-14; 4:1-3, 10-13	17
	Matthew 14:14-21	124
	Hebrews 11:32-34	126
The Shepherd	Psalm 23	98
His 'common sense'	1 Corinthians 1:26-31	78

JESUS

God's Son	Matthew 1:20-25	15
	Matthew 8:23-27	100
	Hebrews 1:1-6	38
His crucifixion	Isaiah 53:4-7	48
	Mark 15:33, 34, 37-39	54

His resurrection	Luke 24:1-8	102
	1 Corinthians 15:12-19	61
He will come again	Matthew 24:3-8	148
	Matthew 24:30-31, 42-44	142
Trusting in Him	Proverbs 3:3-8	45
	Mark 10:13-16	86
	John 20:24-29	20
Our High Priest	Hebrews 4:14-16	134
THE HOLY SPIRIT	Matthew 28:16-20	137
	Luke 22:54-62	56
	John 14:15-19	36
THE CHRISTIAN'S RESPONSIBILITY		
To represent Jesus	John 17:9-19	62
To obey	Joshua 1:1-9	144
	Mark 12:41-44	117
To share their faith	Acts 4:13-15, 18-20	52
To be grateful	Luke 17:11-19	131
To be an influence	Matthew 5:13-16	105
	Acts 5:12-16	94
At home	Luke 8:36-39	121
To care for others	Matthew 25:34-40	42
	John 13:5, 12-15	122
	James 2:14-17	116
The Ten Commandments	Deuteronomy 5:6-21	140-1
Sin	Isaiah 64:4-7	79
	1 Corinthians 10:12-13	133
Prayer	Exodus 17:8-13	58

	Matthew 6:5-13	109
Worship	Romans 12:1, 9-16	108
Love	1 Corinthians 13:1-7	84
The church family	1 Corinthians 12:12-20, 26-27	96
Christian behaviour	Philippians 4:4-9	66
Relationships	1 Kings 11:1-2, 9-11	92
Questions that demand an answer	Mark 8:27-29	150
	John 5:2-9	40
For or against	1 Kings 18:20-21, 36-39	139
A reason to believe	1 Peter 3:13-16	76
	1 John 5:11-15	146
Becoming a Christian	Acts 11:25-26	37
	Revelation 3:20-22	29
A new person	Psalm 40:1-5	22
	Isaiah 64:8-9	120
	Matthew 5:1-12	114
	John 3:1-7	47
	Acts 9:1-6	30
	Romans 6:1-7	74
	Romans 7:15-20	18
	2 Corinthians 5:17-21	82
Life to the full	Matthew 9:10-13	34
	John 10:7-11	67
First priorities	1 Samuel 2:22-25, 30	46
	Amos 5:21-24	136
	Matthew 6:19-21	39
	Matthew 7:24-29	24
	John 3:26-30	110
Right and wrong	Romans 7:21-25	128

	Galatians 5:16-23	106
	Colossians 3:12-24, 23-24	135
Growing up	1 Peter 2:1-3	130
Hope for the future	Jeremiah 29:11-14	72
	John 14:1-6	132
	Revelation 21:2-5	132
Right motives	Matthew 7:21-23	119
	1 Timothy 6:6-10, 17-19	64
Christian commitment	1 Chronicles 28:8-10	118
The cost of being a Christian	Matthew 16:24-27	28
	Luke 9:23-26	149
	Ephesians 6:10-17	127
	1 Timothy 6:11-14	35
	Hebrews 12:1-3	88
	1 Peter 4:12-16	90
All or nothing	Revelation 3:15-19	75
Other gods	Acts 17:16, 19-23	60
Red herrings	1 Timothy 1:3-7	104
Friend of the King	John 15:12-17	49
'I don't know'	1 Corinthians 13:8-13	123

BIBLE INDEX

Exodus 3:10-14; 4:1-3, 10-13	17
Exodus 17:8-13	58
Deuteronomy 5:6-21	140-1
Joshua 1:1-9	144
Joshua 7:20-25	32
1 Samuel 2:22-25, 30	46
1 Kings 11:1-2, 9-11	92
1 Kings 18:20-21, 36-39	139
1 Chronicles 28:8-10	118
Psalm 8:1-5	50
Psalm 23	98
Psalm 40:1-5	22
Psalm 62:1-8	44
Psalm 95:1-7	26
Psalm 139:1-10	111
Proverbs 3:3-8	45
Isaiah 53:4-7	48
Isaiah 64:4-7	79
Isaiah 64:8-9	120
Jeremiah 29:11-14	72
Amos 5:21-24	136
Matthew 1:20-25	15
Matthew 5:1-12	114
Matthew 5:13-16	105
Matthew 6:5-13	109
Matthew 6:19-21	39
Matthew 6:25-34	68
Matthew 7:21-23	119
Matthew 7:24-29	24
Matthew 8:23-27	100
Matthew 9:10-13	34
Matthew 14:14-21	124
Matthew 16:24-27	28
Matthew 22:34-40	91
Matthew 24:3-8	148
Matthew 24:30-31, 42-44	142
Matthew 25:34-40	42

Matthew 28:16-20   137

Mark 8:27-29   150
Mark 10:13-16   86
Mark 12:41-44   117
Mark 15:33-34, 37-39   54

Luke 8:36-39   121
Luke 9:23-26   149
Luke 15:25-32   70
Luke 17:11-19   131
Luke 22:54-62   56
Luke 24:1-8   112

John 3:1-7   47
John 3:13-17   51
John 3:26-30   110
John 5:2-9   40
John 10:7-11   67
John 13:5, 12-15   122
John 14:1-6   132
John 14:15-19   36
John 15:12-17   49
John 17:9-19   62
John 19:28-30   73
John 20:24-29   20

Acts 4:13-15, 18-20   52
Acts 5:12-16   94
Acts 9:1-6   30
Acts 11:25-26   37
Acts 16:25-34   80
Acts 17:16, 19-23   60

Romans 6:1-7   74
Romans 7:15-20   18
Romans 7:21-25   128
Romans 8:28-30   23